THE SECULAR MIND

ROBERT COLES

The Secular Mind

PRINCETON UNIVERSITY PRESS

PRINCETON AND OXFORD

Copyright © 1999 by Princeton University Press
Published by Princeton University Press, 41 William Street,
Princeton, New Jersey 08540
In the United Kingdom: Princeton University Press,
3 Market Place, Woodstock, Oxfordshire OX20 1SY

Fourth printing, and first paperback printing, 2001
Paperback ISBN 0-691-08862-4

*The Library of Congress has cataloged the cloth edition
of this book as follows*

Coles, Robert.
The secular mind / Robert Coles.
p.   cm.
ISBN 0-691-05805-9 (alk. paper)
1. Secularism—United States.   I. Title.
BL2760.C65   1999
291.1′7—dc21   98-39388

This book has been composed in Adobe Garamond

Printed on acid-free paper. ∞

www.pup.princeton.edu

Printed in the United States of America

5   7   9   10   8   6   4

Remembering
Dorothy Day and
Paul Tillich

CONTENTS

Introduction

WHAT follows began in my thinking some four decades ago when I was a resident in child psychiatry at the Children's Hospital in Boston. For various reasons of mind, heart, soul I found myself wanting to be a part of a seminar given by Paul Tillich, who had departed New York City's Union Theological Seminary in order to teach at Harvard University. I still remember the shift in my head as I left a hospital (where the emphasis, even in psychiatry, was on *doing*, on trying to accomplish a specific task) for quite another world, across the Charles River, where we were, as Tillich kept reminding us, "free to let our minds wander," take us where we wanted to go, with no set limits. Again and again our professor would make that distinction for us: the world of action, the world of reflection—and ask us, always, whether the latter qualified as the former. A lot of nit-picking, I sometimes felt. On the other hand, at other moments, I felt so lucky to be able to stop and ponder the meaning of this life—mine, of course, but also that of all of us who for a while exist, go through time, occupy our own infinitesimally small places in the endless space of the universe.

Almost every week Tillich made mention of "the secular mind." I wasn't quite sure what he had in his mind with respect to that kind of mind; nor did he seem interested in defining the phrase. He seemed to assume that we all knew what he meant. I remember wondering one October day, as I rode my bike along the Charles on my way to his seminar, whether "the secular mind" had to do with me then and there going through my motions on wheels, and before that in the hospital, and after that in a classroom: my head responding to necessary tasks, and my head directing my body's actions, and my head in search of—well, "heady stuff" (what a fellow hospital resident of mine chose to call the reading I was doing for that seminar).

Several weeks later, at the end of the class, I decided to approach Tillich, ask him about that phrase "secular mind," because yet again he'd used it. I can still see his broad smile as I put my question to him—and then a surprising response on his part: "I'm sorry, I use the expression too much; it's a theologian's reflex." He must have noticed my unsatisfied, still inquisitive face—and so he went into a disquisition of sorts, which at times I had trouble following, though the heart of it, I surmised, was the distinction he wanted to make between Man the thinking materialist and Man the anxiously aspiring creature who bows his head and prays, and who "looks outside himself to Another, to God," for explanations, understanding, guidance. The foregoing words are, of course, mine, except for the ones in quotation marks, which I remembered hard, wrote down inside the first volume of his *Systematic Theology*, a book we used in his course. For Tillich, I gathered, a secular person was one who looked within himself or herself, within our species, for whatever comprehension of the world is to be found, whereas the sacred mind (he often spoke of our "sacred self," its "search for meaning") looked toward the beyond, toward that "Another," that "God" so often mentioned in our daily lives, that "God" who ironically (Tillich kept reminding us, as had so many others before him, such as Kierkegaard, most powerfully) has become such a part of our secular life—the pietistic reflex (more neurological imagery) as a purveyor of calm, of reassurance, of self-satisfaction. Here is Tillich word-for-word on that score: "Church attendance for us can become a weekly social rite, a boost to our morale." Is that the secular mind in operation? I ventured to inquire. A smile from the professor: "Yes, you have it, there."

I can still visualize that moment—can hear his terse but original way of responding, of using colloquial English, of acknowledging an irony: religious practice as a motion of sorts in the course of ordinary living, as one more exercise of the secular mind. I can also remember myself sitting in a church a month or so afterwards—wondering, courtesy of Professor Tillich, what I was doing there. In fact, I was thinking of that class, of some of its moments, of the above-quoted words. Meanwhile, there was singing and praying and reading from Scripture, even as I had put all of that aside to call upon (if not dote on) my own mind's past experiences as they continued, in a church, to exert their forceful pull on me. It was then, strangely, amidst all the architectural and aesthetic (and, yes, substantive) expression of the sacred (the stained glass windows with their narrative message, the stately hymns, the words spoken from the Old Testament, the New Testament) that I had begun to understand Tillich's "secular mind" in all of its constant ambiguity.

Years later, in New York City, at 36 East First Street, in St. Joseph's House, where Dorothy Day lived, I would hear her use that same phrase, uttering it with a memorable mix of awe, no less, and wry humor. I was tape-recording her comments—an effort on my part to learn about the history of the Catholic Worker Movement. I had spent some time during medical school in a Catholic Worker "hospitality house" but had never really come to a full understanding of that tradition, its intellectual and spiritual underpinnings—so I began to realize in the early 1970s, when I started talking at some length with Dorothy Day, and pursuing the reading she suggested. During one of those meetings, she remarked upon her "secular life"—and continued this way in amplification: "I get so busy doing the things I want to do, love doing, that I forget to ask myself the why of it all; and I forget to ask myself what *might* be, what *ought* be, because I'm in the midst of doing, doing. Thank God for this wonderful secular life—but thank God for giving us a mind that can turn to Him, to ask 'why' and 'wherefore' as well as spend itself to exhaustion getting things done! Some people say to me, 'the secular mind is your enemy.' I say no, no; I say the secular mind is God's huge gift to us, for us to use for the sake of one another, and that way, for His glory. Then, those folks want me to explain myself—and I have to admit, I get cranky, impatient. I want to get on with things—my secular mind working away! But then I'll just be stopped in my tracks. I feel something inside me wanting to express itself: it's me wanting to be on my knees before God and His mystery. That's when your secular thinking stops and your spiritual being takes a front and center place in your life. You're silent and your mind has left you (the 'you' of this life) and it's gone elsewhere, to meet the Lord—somewhere out there, don't ask me where: the secular having a brief time with the sacred. The next minute it's all over; you're back here in full swing."

So she put it, the complexity of our mind's life, the alternations of thinking and doing, of being this and being that, of secular days, sacred moments; and it is in that spirit of hers (she placed herself on the front line of a lived but interrupted secularity) and of Tillich's (in the classroom, he struggled paradoxically to figure out the contemporary, secular manifestations of the sacred) that I try to explore this matter of two minds, our secular thinking and its constant search for moral, if not spiritual, sanction.

I

Secularism in the Biblical Tradition

THROUGHOUT the history of Christianity the authority of the sacred has never been taken for granted as a compelling moral and spiritual given of unassailable sway. Indeed, the lives of the saints have borne continuing witness to the vulnerability of religious faith, its bouts of frailty in the face of this or that era's challenges. Hence the word secular: the things of a particular time. Such worldliness need not be aggressively ideological, a philosophy that directly takes on a belief in God, a lived commitment to principles and practices upheld in His (or Her or Its) name. The issue, rather, has commonly been regarded (and in letters, essays, books pronounced) as psychological rather than cultural or sociological: the tug, seemingly inevitable, of our senses, our appetites, upon the direction of our energies. God awaits us, as do the various houses of worship that insist upon and celebrate the primacy of the sacred, yet we yield to or seek outright the profane: ideas and values and habits and interests that have their origin in our earthly lives, our day-to-day desires, worries, frustrations, resentments.

Saint Paul (arguably the first Christian theologian) stressed the rock-bottom implacability of such secularism: its hold on us that stretches over all generations—until, that is, we are back to God's first chosen two, the man Adam, the woman Eve, both nakedly unselfconscious and under no threat of disappearance, extinction.

Secularism was born in that fabled "garden" of yore, when curiosity spawned knowledge. The first secularist, in a sense, was the serpent who is described as "subtle" (still no small virtue among many of us unashamed heathens), and who egged Eve on all too persuasively. In no time she and Adam were having quite a time of it—and the result, really, was the mythical birth of the mind as we know it today, countless centuries later. "The eyes of them both were opened"—a clear, sometimes scary awareness of themselves, of the world around them, of space and time: the intellect that peers, pokes, pries. But that intellect (those opened eyes) right away had to contend with a rush of emotion, an altogether new notion of themselves: "They knew that they were naked, and they sewed fig leaves together and made themselves aprons." Here is the first recorded instance of shame, and its consequences; here is a physical act (the sewing of leaves) as an expression of an inner state of alarm, regret, fear. Immediately thereafter such apprehension, prompted by an awareness of wrongdoing, is enacted, given dramatic expression: "And they heard the voice of the Lord God walking in the garden in the cool of the day; and Adam and his wife hid themselves from the presence of the Lord God amongst the trees of the garden."

Soon enough those two, now mere mortals, and so destined to die, are headed "east of Eden," where their descendants (all of us) would try to make the best of a bad deal: a major transgression had elicited a swift, unrelenting punishment (of a kind that is utterly defining both psychologically and physically), and a kind of careless abandon, as a birthright, had been taken away, replaced by suffering and more suffering, though with a new kind of mental activity, driven by an acquired moral energy (what happened when that forbidden "tree of the knowledge of good and evil" lost its aura of inaccessibility).

In the biblical chapters that follow the expulsion of Adam and Eve from the Lord's terrain, so to speak, much is made of the consequent and subsequent physical hardship, pain: floods and pestilence and drought; the hunger and illness that accompanied them. But there was, too, the subjectivity that this new life brought: human beings as exiles, as wanderers, as people paying (forever, it seemed) a price for an act of disobedience, a severe transgression that carried with it the death penalty. That inner state was, right off, marked by self-preoccupation—another first, that of a necessary narcissism as a requirement for a creature suddenly at the mercy of the elements, and with a fixed span of time available. True, after the Flood, the Lord (in Exodus) relents a bit, promises not to be persecutory in the extreme—hence the survival of humankind. But death is our fate, still. We are left to fend for ourselves, and to do so with apprehension either a constant presence or around any corner. But we are also left with a steadily increasing capacity to make the best of our fatefully melancholy situation: the freedom, and need, to explore, to experiment, to master as best we can what we see and touch. We are left, too, after that terrible Flood of six centuries duration, with a negotiation of sorts: "And God blessed Noah and his sons, and said unto them, be fruitful and multiply, and replenish the earth." A newly generous turn on the Lord's part: those people once described as "fugitives and vagabonds" were entrusted with their own earthly sovereignty. An agreement was reached, and our secular rights, privileges were affirmed: "And the fear of you and the dread of you shall be upon every beast of the earth, and upon every fowl of the air, upon all that moveth upon the earth, and upon all the fishes of the sea; into your hand are they delivered." In vivid imagery God is said to have spelled out His promise—the so-called covenant of the rainbow, a partial retraction of an earlier curse, with the implication that an ingenious humankind can survive, if it pays heed to the environment, uses it as required.

But of course the Lord did not match His gift of a subservient outside world with an offer to subdue the minds and hearts and souls of this first among creatures. Put differently, covenantal Judaism addressed our progressive triumph over a raw, threatening, potentially destructive Nature yet gave us no leeway over our thinking and feeling life. Animals can be our prey, but the animal in us prowls mightily or stealthily, as the case may be.

Not that God lost interest in our attitudes, in what we held dear, and why. The God of the Hebrew Bible is repeatedly observant and testing. One moment He seems ready to let this big shot among "living things" simply be in charge, have a time of it on the planet; another time He concentrates His moral sights on us, wants to make sure we know how interested He is in how we behave, in what we believe, and, not least, in how we regard Him. This latter supposition about God—proposed by, among others, the twentieth-century theologian Karl Barth, who saw *Him* as a seeker—by implication plays into our secular life: we are desirable enough to earn His constant interest. Our self-preoccupations are affirmed by His preoccupation with us, and that egoism (or, these days, narcissism) amounts to a veiled variant of secularism: the self of the here and now in all its ceaselessly sought affirmations, in this instance one buttressed by theology, no less.

Before Barth, there was Søren Kierkegaard, who was no stranger to psychology, even if he preferred to use it as a means of understanding our search for moral meaning, rather than our search for the less obvious, if not hidden, sides of ourselves. Kierkegaard, unlike many intellectual contemporaries of his, took seriously not only the story of Jesus but the Hebrew Bible as well—and not only the prophetic (or later) Judaism of Isaiah, Jeremiah, Amos, Micah, but the founding moments, they might be called, of that hugely demanding monotheistic faith. In *Fear and Trembling*, for instance, we are asked to consider Abraham's walk up a mountain in "the land of Moriah" with his beloved son Isaac. There God has sought him out in an apparently merciless (and inscrutable) way: the demand that a father kill his son as evidence of a compliant faith. Here are words of high drama, of staggering anxiety: "Take now thy son [The Lord insists], thine only son Isaac, whom thou lovest . . . and offer him . . . for a burnt offering upon one of the mountains which I will tell thee of. . . . And they came to the place which God had told him of; and Abraham built an altar there, and laid the wood in order; and bound Isaac his son, and laid him on the altar upon the wood. And Abraham stretched forth his hand, and took the knife to slay his son." Suddenly, though, the "angel of the Lord" calls from Heaven, tells Abraham to stop in his tracks, to spare his son, "for now I know that thou fearest God, seeing thou has not withheld thy son, thine only son from me."

For Kierkegaard such a moment was charged with a kind of moral irony almost beyond analysis or even description through man's distinctive gift, the use of words. Not that he didn't try—*Fear and Trembling* won't let go of Abraham and his willingness to follow God's direction, no matter the cost to himself, his wife Sarah, their son, Isaac. We are given, at one point, a metaphysician's abstract summary, a concept to keep in mind: "the teleological suspension of the ethical"—an occasion where our sense of right and wrong, even our ordinary sense of what we simply never could or would do, is forsaken in favor of an ascent toward a faith ultimately challenged (as opposed to a descent to the most brutish kind of criminality, callousness). For Kierkegaard our ordinary ethical standards don't apply when God calls, though in anyone's contemporary daily life (so it has been for a long time!) such an explicit summons from the Lord, or that "angel" of his possessed of speech, seems quite beyond the bounds of possibility. In a less theoretical vein, however, Kierkegaard leaves ethical contemplation for a simpler, more accessible (and affecting) narrative mode: "By faith Abraham went from the land of his fathers and became a sojourner in the land of promise. He left one thing behind, took one thing with him: he left his earthly understanding behind and took faith with him—otherwise he would not have wandered forth but would have thought this unreasonable."

Secularism is thereby acknowledged in its obviously compelling attraction—precisely the target of a God intent on a mind-boggling insistence: toss aside the loftiest of the secular, the commonsense family ties that, actually, are the bottom line, morally, for so many of us. No wonder, in Elie Wiesel's *Night* the full brunt of the Nazi horror as it got enacted in those concentration camps is realized when we learn of a boy's eventual indifference to his own father, a storyteller's personal acknowledgment that the most personal of ties, those that develop in a family, had been shattered in this precipitous downward moral collapse. But for Abraham the action was all upward: the climbing of a mountain, the hearing of a message from the heavens, the seemingly quick responsiveness on his part (he becomes a "sojourner in the land of promise"). The matter at hand, Kierkegaard reminds us, is a "heinous sin," and yet in some fashion (and without discussion or reflection) the man and husband and father Abraham becomes, with apparent effortlessness, a "knight of faith." Whence this "infinite resignation" that translated into a hand poised with a knife, ready to plunge it into a son's body? Here is a further irony: "Those . . . who carry the jewel of faith are likely to be delusive, because their outward appearance bears a striking resemblance to that which both the infinite resignation and faith profoundly despise . . . to Philistinism."

We know from Kierkegaard's *This Present Age* the posture he could summon for the philistine—the satirist's biting scorn. In that relatively brief essay he takes on, really, the Danish (and by extension European) bourgeoisie of his time, the restless yearnings of people who may go to church on Sunday for an hour or so, but who live strongly attached to a shifting assortment of possessions, projects, plans: things to own, things to do, things to dream of accomplishing. He notices the boredom that attends such activity, as if the secular world, in itself, provides little real inspiration to those who live there. Yet the alternative, a thoroughgoing commitment to the sacred, is beyond the imagining, let alone the aspiration, of most of us (certainly including, he says over and over, the multitude of professed Christians whose vows of loyalty to God, to Jesus, are regularly, loudly spoken). Indeed, for Kierkegaard organized Christianity, Catholic and Protestant alike, is one more aspect of the "philistinism," the prosaic secularism that he so evidently disdains. He needn't deign to remind us of the medieval Catholic Church, or the fat and sassy Protestant burghers whom he, a minister's son, knew by common sight. He assumes secularism as the mainstay of the Christian life for many centuries, even as he assumes that Abraham was no saintly creature, abruptly rewarded by a grateful God.

The historical surprise of a flawed father walking with his son to a destination that seemed all too final for the father, as he contemplated it, is meant to give us pause, still—no matter who we are, where or when we live. As for Isaac, we're never told what he knew, if anything, as he walked so trustingly alongside Abraham. Kierkegaard insists, though, that this was not a pair that could be quickly singled out, declared the winners of a divine moral sweepstakes: God's chosen (and most exceptional) spiritual combatants. Rather, he clothes them in a secular garb, even back then, several millennia before his time. In a sense, then, he is reprimanding his own caustic tongue, telling us that sociology and psychology, infant "sciences" in the middle of the nineteenth century, would be of no help in singling out a "knight of faith"; nor is there a course of study, or, alas, a religious practice, that secures for somebody such a spiritual station or "level" of success. Paradoxically, the secular can mask (that is, contain) the sacred—hence the mystery of faith, which Kierkegaard, with no embarrassment whatever, keeps trying to uphold, notwithstanding his cleverly modern, introspectively astute, socially watchful and discerning mind.

Kierkegaard attends carefully to Abraham's relationship with God precisely because in that encounter the assumptions of rational secularism are directly confronted, dismissed. *Fear and Trembling* takes on nineteenth-century romanticism and enlightenment, both, with a vengeance: "Abraham is therefore at no instant a tragic hero, but something quite different, either a murderer or a believer." True, by virtue of the absurd, Isaac is not at the last moment sacrificed—a decision, however, of God's, not Abraham's. We who consider that story have no real way of presuming to put ourselves in Abraham's shoes and can only, these days, "play" with such a story intellectually, as Kierkegaard did. Yet it is a biblical story and was meant to tell a sacred lesson to early secularists: God's ways are not ours, hence "fear and trembling" as a worthy response to that event, rather than an effort, say, of historical (or moral) analysis.

The thrust of Kierkegaard's essay is the unyielding disparity between the sacred and the secular. If Abraham had to surrender his son in a gesture of faith, we readers (of the Bible or of a brilliant and cranky nine-teenth-century Danish theologian) have to surrender our usual (secular) assumptions about what matters and why when we try to make sense of a world utterly else-where. Nor was Kierkegaard unaware that a similar pre-dicament confronted those who lived in Palestine when Jesus walked that land, taught and healed and exhorted the multitude—only to be killed in the company of thieves.

But between the time of Abraham's encounter with God on one mountain, and the time of Jesus as he preached and prophesied on another, there were addi-tional efforts to confront the Jewish people with the de-mands of faith, none more important, of course, than that of Moses, who also went up a mountain to hear God's wishes—and did so at greater length, surely, than anyone else mentioned in the Bible. For pages in Scrip-ture we learn of those conversations: they are true ex-changes, and on occasion the lowly mortal one takes issue with his Lord, even turns Him around, gets Him to see things differently. Indeed, Moses and God collab-orate together, plan a strategy meant to tame morally a people, bring them convincingly the Ten Command-ments, of course, also bring them all sorts of other in-structions, commands, announcements, recommenda-tions. Moses is always called the great lawgiver of his people, but he was also a negotiator of sorts, a trusted emissary of no less than God, and, not least, an inter-preter of the sacred for the secularist crowds of his time. He was, in that regard, a master of the details and habits and rituals that make up ordinary life; and he was constantly intent on shaping the way his fellow Jews lived their daily lives, in the hope that a people singled out by the Lord would, finally, dedicate themselves to Him in just the ways He wished.

No question he was, in secular terms, a "great man," or a "leader"—hence Freud's desire, in *Moses and Monotheism*, to see him as the victim of parricide, a conclusion that tells a lot about a particular theorist's unrelenting determination to see things his way at all costs. Not that Freud was the first one to take the Moses story and fit it to his secular requirements. During Moses' long life (he reputedly died at 120) he surely incurred the resistance of many: the Decalogue he transmitted to his people is a demanding call to God's ways, a rebuke to man's inclinations, impulses. Moses gave his fellow Jews a divinely sanctioned collective conscience; though if there was anxiety and anger, as a consequence, there was surely the gratitude that goes with a clear-cut mandate proclaimed in the name of the highest possible authority. Here was an unequivocal monotheism, but also rules about daily living, the rights and wrongs of it. An ancient kind of secularism was confronted head-on: the great man has heard, again and again, the word of God, and in His name (not that of some tribal seer or chief) has spoken out loud and strong.

Yet even God's direct message, conveyed through a chosen intermediary (himself commanding, intriguing, a savvy but principled spokesman and negotiator) will wane in its capacity to convince, exert control. The prophetic Judaism of Jeremiah, especially, bears witness to the betrayal of covenantal Judaism at the hands of a people become all too spiritually indifferent, if not callous. The intensity of Jeremiah's denunciations (the first jeremiads!) measures the moral decline of a people, their embrace of what is convenient, momentarily satisfying: the self-indulgence of the temporal order. "Run ye to and fro through the streets of Jerusalem," the great social and cultural critic exhorts, anxious that those who read/hear his words become aware of inequity in all its garbs and disguises abroad the land. But this is a condemnation, a remonstrance in the name of religion: "Therefore, I am full of the fury of the Lord." The prophet speaks, as Moses before him, in His name: "The word that came to Jeremiah from the Lord, saying. . . . " A society gone secular, forgetful of God-given rules, laws, commandments, is vigorously chastised— and not abstractly. Repeatedly calling upon direct observation, Jeremiah is a documentarian of distant yore who regards closely and firsthand a particular fallen world: "Seest not what they do in the cities of Judah and in the streets of Jerusalem?" These are words of spiritual alarm and dismay directed with righteous vehemence and near despair: "Oh that my head were waters, and mine eyes a fountain of tears, that I might weep day and night for the slain of the daughter of my people."

As the caustic essayist or aroused moralist lets loose his scorn, he renders by implication a portrait of long ago secularism worthy of one of today's gloomy naysayers, grievously upset by a moral decline in this or that nation's public or private life. To be sure, some of our social observers are reluctant to betray even mild indignation, let alone outrage—a measure of the distance, with respect to moral conviction, that their readers/

listeners have traveled since Jeremiah's time. The lyrical heat in his statements, the raw passion he harnesses to his denunciations of an ancient secularism, tells us a lot about not only him but his intended audience: these are people corrupted, but within hearing distance, it can be said, of the very spiritual voices that were so evidently, flagrantly unheeded. In our time, among many who regard themselves as well educated and, too, philosophically inclined, ethically awake, a moralist of Jeremiah's rhetorical persuasion might be readily dismissed as all too caught up in his own "problems"—if not plain loony. Moreover, much of our influential social criticism is, naturally, secular in nature: the writer or speaker draws upon a particular civic or intellectual tradition. A good number of those who resemble Jeremiah in their words, their tone, are for many of us "fundamentalists," no compliment, despite the prime meaning of the word; or again, are consigned to the ranks of the mentally unsettled or worse.

Secularism links our age with Zion as it edged toward the time of Jesus Christ. His kind of life, for millions of us (at least in creedal expression) a continuation of prophetic Judaism, and more, a culmination of it, was unacceptable to the people of His time, and the same fate can await many who labor spiritually today. In this regard, I'd best jump from the Galilee wherein Jesus lived, spoke, to the Lower East Side in Manhattan in 1973, where Dorothy Day, a journalist, political activist, novelist, and onetime companion drinker to the likes of Eugene O'Neill, Mike Gold, John Dos Passos, Malcolm Cowley, reminisced about the perception of her that suddenly arose among some of her old friends, never mind various strangers: "I lived a Greenwich Village life for a long time. I wrote for liberal and radical journals. I didn't completely like being called 'serious,' but it was meant as a compliment. I'd gone to jail [as a suffragette] and I'd criticized the country for its indifference to the poor—and my friends encouraged me and told me I was doing a good job. When I started saying the same things, actually, but in the name of God—well, that was a different matter altogether! The first wave of disbelief took the form of worry: was I *all right*? It's hard to fight *that* one! What do you do—ask if the person who is speaking those words is *all right*? Not if you're trying to invoke the Jesus who prayed to the Lord that He forgive those who were mocking Him! I began to realize that in our secular world there's plenty of room for social or cultural criticism, so long as it is secular in nature. But I'd crossed the street, you could say; I'd gone over to those crazy ones, who speak—well, one of my old drinking friends (he taught at Columbia) called it 'God talk.' He said to me once: 'Dorothy, why do you now need "God talk" to lay into America for all its wrongs? You used to do a great job when you were a muckraking reporter, with no "religion" sandwiched into your writing.'"

By then Dorothy Day was hopelessly, in her own words (the enemy's line of thought embraced!) "a fool for Christ"—and therein a twentieth-century echo of what Jeremiah and his kind must have heard, and, to a pitch of frenzy, Jesus of Nazareth, also, as he became more and more soul-stirred, more and more skeptical of prevailing principalities and powers, and willing to take them on directly or by analogy. Those parables of his were meant to hit the listener hard, give him or her plenty of reason to look askance at what passed for the popular, the conventional, the regular or customary. What to make of one who remarks that "the last shall be first, the first last": a direct slam at secular accomplishment and power, a direct embrace of the lowly, of people more than occasionally regarded as lazy, incompetent, or worse by those on the top? What to make, further, of the company Jesus kept: those fisherman and peasants, those sick ones, hurt ones, those scorned and rebuked ones? What to make, finally, of his considerable nerve: he who invoked the Lord regularly, and who spoke in His name?

No matter one's decision with regard to Christ's eventual divinity, while here on earth for a short thirty-three years he regularly took issue, we can surely agree, with the secular world of a powerful (Roman) empire in the name of the sacred. He was a spiritually aroused itinerant storyteller, a moral evangelist of humble background, who for a while attracted a large following, probably the reason for his undoing at the hands of those with political power. Nor did he endear himself to those of his own people who had religious power; he was, in a sense, a reform Jew deeply troubled by what he saw, heard in the temple: shades of Jeremiah, of course. His death was a secular one, at the hands of the state: the doing-in of a spiritually possessed young man who came to Jerusalem, a country boy, one might say—with an accent that bespoke lowliness, with no connections to the mighty, the influential, and with a record of fomenting a kind of civil unrest. His speech was unsettling in tone, if not specific word: "I come to bring you

not peace, but the sword." He did, indeed, seem to
want to cut a swath through the everyday assumptions
of a people now under the imperial sway of generals and
their lieutenants who were hardly interested in, sympa-
thetic to Judaism, its monotheism, its long-standing
ethical traditions, so intimately connected to its history.
Jesus was not the first nor the last critic of that empire's
values (or of his own people's moral subjugation—his
target rather than their political servitude) to be killed.
Rome was not Nazi Germany or Stalin's Russia, but it
knew how to enforce its sovereignty; and so, years after
Jesus had died, when his followers persisted in speaking
in his name, living in accordance with his precepts,
they, too, were done away with, fed to devouring animals, some of them, rather than strung up on a cross.

All of that—the stuff of the Christian legend as it
has survived across two millennia—would soon enough
be institutionalized (hence the undiminished collective
memory of a seemingly obscure and unsurprising moment in the day-to-day history of a far-flung empire's
provincial life). Put differently, Jesus and his followers
preceded by several generations what became Christianity: an inspired and inspiring spiritual figure, who took
on a particular secular world, became in a century or
two the Son of God, with buildings dedicated to the
perpetuation of His name and His words, and with men
and women spending their lives doing likewise in those
buildings and elsewhere. But in no time that sacred mission, that organization (with rules and regulations and a
proclaimed moral and spiritual authority) itself became
very much part of the secular world—to the point that,
in the Middle Ages, the Holy Roman Catholic Church

had become in many respects an empire: rich, complacent, a player in all the intrigues of the day. Thereupon, of course, the arrival of the latter-day Jeremiahs, the necessary scolds, who railed at corruption and degradation of all kinds at the highest levels of so-called sacred communities, in the Vatican and elsewhere. But such criticism, from within or without, can't banish the essential historical irony, that in the name of an initial spiritual remonstrance of established secular and sacred power, an institution of great influence emerged, and with that development, a new kind of secularism: bishops and popes sitting down with kings and queens, and, later, lay leaders of all kinds, to decide about all sorts of secular matters.

In protest of Rome's moral corruption, a Luther would rise to say no, to demand a more rigorous adherence to the sacred. But he, too, sat with secular leaders, and in fact Lutheranism would take the proclaimed sanctity of Christianity into a new domain of the secular: the church as a pillar of the nation-state's authority. No wonder Dietrich Bonhoeffer's special agony: he saw right away Hitler's hateful secularism, but he, a Lutheran, saw his fellow Lutheran pastors embrace that version of secularism, wrap themselves in the swastika, even in the brown shirts of the street thugs who had run interference (and worse) for the rising, Austrian-born demagogue. In the end, Bonhoeffer took aim not only at Hitler but at Lutheranism as it came to such easy terms with him—the supposedly sacred proving itself, in the name of *realpolitik*, the merely secular.

Such an accommodation may strike us as disgraceful because of the morally grotesque nature of Nazism;

whereas we blink at, or simply fail to notice, the less dramatic accommodations that take place in our own more "civilized" countries, cultures. Here, for example, is Bonhoeffer writing from a concentration camp in the last year of his life (Hitler would have him killed in April of 1945, a few weeks before his own suicide):

> There still remain the so-called "ultimate questions"—death, guilt—to which only "God" can give an answer, and because of which we need God and the Church and the pastor. So we live, in some degree, on these so-called ultimate questions of humanity. But what if one day they no longer exist as such, if they too can be answered "without God"? Of course, we now have the secularized offshoots of Christian theology, namely existentialist philosophy and psychotherapists, who demonstrate to secure, contented, and happy mankind that it is really unhappy and desperate and simply unwilling to admit that it is in a predicament about which it knows nothing, and from which only they can rescue it. Wherever there is health, strength, security, simplicity, they send luscious fruit to gnaw at or to lay their pernicious eggs in. They set themselves to drive people to inward despair, and then the game is in their hands. That is secularized methodism.

The words of a prisoner who knew that death might be around any corner, and so, arguably, an exaggerated or overwrought take on those philosophers and psychologists. Still, Bonhoeffer knew that both Heidegger and Jung had made a kind of peace with the Nazis that he judged contemptible on Christian grounds, and, as already noted, he knew that the overwhelming majority of German Christendom, not to mention that nation's professoriat and its psychological healers, both lay and medical, had done likewise. From a privileged Aryan family, he might have had it otherwise, avoided the fate of an active opponent of the Nazis. Indeed, in the summer of 1939 he was in America—a visiting scholar at Union Theological Seminary, where he could have stayed through the war and where he was already celebrated for his strong, outspoken resistance to Hitler. (Bonhoeffer went on the radio to criticize Germany's "Führer" two days after President von Hindenberg made his fateful decision to appoint Adolf Hitler the Reich's chancellor, and the pastor was cut off as he tried to warn his listeners of the terrible consequences ahead for them, for their Christian faith.) As a matter of fact, when this young and already distinguished theologian decided to return to Germany, to continue to take his quite dangerous stand against the Nazis, he was himself regarded a candidate for the "help" of those very psychotherapists whom he would mention a few years later with no great admiration. In Reinhold Niebuhr's succinct words: "We worried about him; we knew how endangered he'd be, if he returned—but he *had* to go back: he was a deeply religious man, one who took Christ's life to heart, and tried to live up to it."

By the end of his life Bonhoeffer, the onetime cosmopolitan Berliner, a Lutheran in his early career by conviction, had left churchgoing for something quite else, the "Christian life" Niebuhr was trying to describe. This fearlessly decent religious philosopher and pastor, this promising scholar whose books had achieved considerable and favorable attention, felt at an utter remove from his nation's policies, practices, and thoroughly disenchanted, disgusted by his church's collaborative engagement with what he regarded as the Devil itself, the Antichrist. As one reads his late diary entries and the books he wrote against the darkening shadows of Hitler's consolidation of brute power (in the late 1930s), such as *The Cost of Discipleship*, one is carried back in time to the earliest years of the so-called Christian Era: to the "Christian life" lived by Jesus himself, and his band of followers, who risked so very much for what they held dear.

Put differently, Bonhoeffer refused the choice of exile (a step many fellow clergymen and intellectuals willingly took) because his values weren't secular. He did not, in the end, regard himself as a university teacher, as a minister, as a book-writing intellectual, as a cultivated person of many gifts and passions (he played the piano exceedingly well, wrote poetry), all of which he most certainly was—but rather as a disciple of Jesus Christ who had the responsibility and wish to risk everything, his life included, in pursuit of what Jesus (become the Christ) proclaimed, urged, died in seeking: the sanctity of faith enacted in the here, the now of a lived life. I never heard the matter put better, actually, than as Professor David Roberts, who taught at Union Theological Seminary in the 1950s, did when he tried to describe Bonhoeffer's last days and, before them, his commitments that proved fatal to him: "He lived as a *homo religiosus*, and he died a Christian martyr. There were others who died fighting the Nazis—or openly fought them in Germany, and then fled. But they were secular heroes. Even among the clergy who said no to the

Nazis—a small number, sad to say—few were as bold as Bonhoeffer. His lack of discretion tells the full story: he wasn't operating on the principles that govern most of us (practicality, probability of success in what you're trying to do, and the chances for survival); he was fulfilling a sacred calling, not making the sober and sane calculations of a secular life."

A pause—and then an afterthought put in the form of a question, which does haunting justice to a haunting Christian witness that ended on April 9, 1945, in the Flossenburg concentration camp: "People often ask what the rest of us are to make of him [Bonhoeffer], of what he did, but I wonder whether we ought not ask ourselves what his life has to teach us about *ourselves*, about how we behave and what we believe and what we do (if anything!) to indicate that what we really believe has much to do with how we live." Further on in a conversation powerfully instructive, Professor Roberts reminded us of what by then had become obvious, courtesy of his commentary, though the way he put it was original, so we students thought then, and so I still think as I remember a professor's words, written down: "God is timeless, and so is faith, and so is doubt— Bonhoeffer in his heart and mind and soul became one of the disciples of Jesus; [thereby] he jumped over all those centuries."

History tempts us, naturally, to think otherwise, and so do psychology and sociology: we all live in a particular place and time. We wonder about Bonhoeffer's emotional life, or his family's values, or the particular German philosophical and spiritual idealism that inspired him. As for his stalwart capacity to endure Nazi harassment, threats, punishment, confinement, and the constant threat of death—surely the tinge of bitterness and melancholy in his letters bespeaks a mind under severe strain, a mind trying hard to sustain itself "adaptively" in the face of a naked terror constantly exerted. But Professor Roberts wanted us to pose another possibility: that our manner of regarding Bonhoeffer was inadequate, to say the least, although thoroughly revealing about ourselves rather than the intended "subject" of scrutiny. We were, really, trying to comprehend a life fueled by spiritual energy through a way of thinking that had little to do with religious ideals as they get turned, by some, into intensely guiding principles: secular minds unable to fathom the workings (the assumptions, the yearnings, the expectations, and, yes, the worries and fears) of a mind tied significantly to the sacred.

I believe that Bonhoeffer did, indeed, leap over nineteen hundred years, embrace those desert wanderers who belonged to, not a church, an institution, a sect, but a community of kindred souls; and in a way I only began to understand what happened to him in the Delta of Mississippi in 1964, during the height of the civil rights struggle, when I was working in a so-called Freedom House in Canton, and talking with, among others, a black man, Joseph Gaines, who had wanted for years to be a minister, but who was, instead, a tenant farmer. Moreover, he was no mean critic of the very church life he sought out so hungrily on Sundays, as he once let me know in this way: "I'll be praying to Jesus, and I'll feel Him right beside me. No, He's inside me, that's it. I think the church people, they want you to come visit them, and that way you meet the Lord, and

His Boy, His Son. The trouble is, you leave, and the Lord and Jesus stay—they don't go with you. You go back to being yourself, in the state of Mississippi, in the United States of America, and it's 1964, and you've got the bills to pay, and you've got the church to pay, too— a donation every Sunday, yes sir! So, I say to myself: be on your own with God—He can be your friend all the time, not just Sunday morning. Come Monday and Tuesday and through the week to meet Him in church, or go find Him some other place—He's everywhere, if you'll only want to look. If you live with Him long and hard, you're carrying His spirit; if you think of Him but once a week you're just another—I guess you be another Mississippian!

"I'd like to be a minister, so I could know the Bible, and preach it to other folks. But in my heart, I don't believe the Lord wants me preaching on Sundays; He wants me living His way all the days of the week. I recall being little, and I asked my Pa [his grandfather] why it was that Jesus lived so long ago, and here we are, so far from where He was, the distance away, and the time, too. 'Joe,' he said, 'you got it all wrong. He is here, right near you, right inside you—if you want Him to be.' 'Sure,' I said; 'you bet,' I said; 'wow, yes sir,' I said—I want Him as near as can be. But Pa told me not so fast, young one; he told me that He's with you if you earn the right for Him to be there, and if you don't, then He's not, and you can go to church and put money in the basket and pray your head off and sing your voice out until it's gone and said good-bye, and still He won't be paying you mind, because—that's it!—you're not paying Him any mind, and it's a two-way street, sure is.

"On a good day, when I've remembered Jesus, by the way I am with my family and friends, then I'm sure He's smiling and saying, you're with Me, yes sir; on a bad day, when I'm all pouty and mean in my manners, then He's gone on to find the good souls to keep company with, and I'm just here, alone, figuring out how I can take care of mister Me, and not caring about others, and isn't that the first stop on the bus headed for hell!"

As I heard those words, I remembered Reinhold Niebuhr and David Roberts telling us students that when Bonhoeffer was at Union Theological Seminary (like Simone Weil when she was in New York), he went to Harlem to church—not in order to try to be of help to the poor, to people long humiliated, but in the conviction that Jesus was to be found there, rather than at the seminary, or the churches in the fancy parts of Manhattan. Well, of course, who is to say exactly where God is to be found? Yet, as that humble yeoman was trying to suggest, the Lord may indeed be anywhere, everywhere, may have visited people and places at all times. For some, though, He is a companion, a daily guide, whereas for others, a presence, a high presence, to be visited occasionally, be it weekly or on holidays only: a life bent on passing a kind of constant sacred muster or a life predominantly secular in its commitments. For Joseph Gaines, for Dietrich Bonhoeffer, Paul's conversion on the road to Damascus or Jeremiah's furious lamentations are not at all a far distant moment, reported in Scripture as a part of ancient history, but the stuff of daily living, without which secularity soon enough asserts its thrust, its lure, as has happened all the time and in all possible places, including, of course, the

Vatican, this or that abbey in England, the churches where hymns are sung in memory of Martin Luther.

Nor has secularism over the centuries (and within the biblical tradition) been a matter only of sin or temptation or simple acquiescence in all that plentifully *is*. As R. H. Tawney in *Religion and the Rise of Capitalism* and Max Weber in *The Protestant Ethic and the Spirit of Capitalism* have reminded us, and as Ignazio Silone likewise did, as a storyteller rather than a social theorist, religious tradition can very much connect with, even stir strongly, a secular society, give it a cadre of "believers" who work their hearts out—feverish in their compliance with business and government officials, desperately eager in their wish to show themselves godly by proving themselves, without letup, willing workers. It was, perhaps, easier for Bonhoeffer to take on (take after) the intelligentsia, the *haute bourgeoisie* of his native Germany, or for that matter, of England and the United States or Spain, three countries in which he lived for months at a time, than to take note of the ordinary working people of those countries, of any country: men and women who every day show up for work in factories, offices, whether in blue or white collars. True, for so many of us there is no choice: one works or one goes hungry. Still, the mind not only succumbs to secular necessity; the mind can make the best of a tough ordeal, even (as the saying goes) a bad thing.

"I won't tell you I'm in heaven when I'm there on the [assembly] line," a man who works in a General Electric factory in Lynn, Massachusetts, tells me in July 1972, but then follows a description of his daily efforts that shows me how sacred themes in a culture can exert themselves to the advantage of a predominantly secular life: "My both parents were—they called themselves 'God-fearing,' and they *were*! My dad would say, He's watching you, son, so you better try your best. Those three words ring in my ear to this very day, and I'm getting near a half century old: *try your best.* I guess I do. I show up early and leave late. I clock in the hours—and I bring home the bacon: that's life. Sundays, in church, I'll hear about all the troubles that came His way, to Jesus, and I say to myself: hey mister, He was the Son of God, that's what He was, and look at all that happened to Him. Can you imagine, being nailed up like that, and no one giving a hoot or a holler about you—everybody even calling you bad names? No way to end your life—He was a young man! The lesson: don't feel sorry for yourself! Don't slack off in self-pity—my mom told us four [him and his brother and two sisters] that all the time, and she got it right. So, [while on the job] I think of the sermon or one of the hymns, and I try to keep on my toes. 'Step on it!'—I'll say that to myself, sometimes out loud. You know, I'm not kidding myself: I'm just a two-bit worker in a big plant, but I'm better off than way over half the folks on this planet—hell, 90 percent, I'll bet—and it hurts me bad (kills me!) to think that I've had it easier here in this life than Jesus Christ Almighty did, the few years He came to spend with us. Go figure it out!"

After a fashion, he himself has managed to figure it all out—settle in his mind his own responsibilities as a husband, father, provider, and worker, even an employee: "I try to leave my spot [where he stands] clean, and I'll cut back on a break, if it's best for our [assembly

line] team." He has also managed to connect his everyday life to his sense of what truly matters, not through a
showy, talkative, self-regarding, and smug insistence on
his religious faith, and not, certainly, through efforts to
corral others to his way of thinking, but rather through
resort to memory, meditation, observation. That is,
he remembers the strongly held and asserted religious
values of his parents, become his own; he calls up passages of the Bible in an effort to make sense of his personal life, his life as a worker; and he uses his biblical
knowledge as a lens of sorts, through which he takes in
what he sees in such a way that he obtains a coherent
picture of what is happening around him. ("I'll be driv-
ing, and something will happen—a guy is acting crazy
with his car, passing, passing, and I'll remember Jesus
saying, 'What profiteth?' and it all makes sense."). A
worker's secular life gains coherence through his persisting connection to the sacred. His imaginative life even
draws on the stained glass windows of the church he
attends, the illustrations of the books his children read
in Sunday school: "I can put myself over there [in ancient Palestine] in my head—I'll be listening to Jesus
give one of His talks, along with all the other folks. No,
I hadn't thought how I'd look—be dressed [I had
asked]. I guess I'm invisible to all of them; that's how it
goes [in his thinking], or else they'd all notice me." In a
humble, stoic, persevering life a mind crosses time and
space to find the sacred, bring it home to a particular
secularity.

Not that such a person is, to use Emerson's phrase,
"representative man." He is the first to distinguish himself (not in a self-serving manner) from many of his

coworkers and neighbors: "Different people have different things they think of—in their spare time, when they've got time to think." Here, unpretentiously, he knows to skirt the temptation to generalize; rather, he aims to uphold a concreteness worthy of Husserl's repeated phenomenological assertion of human particularity. Still, he makes it amply clear that in the late twentieth century he belongs, to a significant degree, in the company of those who died in the first century. Sometimes, when he confesses to his "failures," to falling short of his spiritual ideals, to a quiet perplexity at what he sees around him (on television, in movies, in newspaper and magazine advertisements), I dare link him in my thoughts to Pietro da Morrone, the Benedictine hermit monk who was summoned to Rome in 1294, turned into a pope—Celestino V. In no time (a mere five months) he had abdicated, his luminous inwardness and piety, his lifelong sanctity, no help at all in dealing with the demands of papal politics. When a General Electric factory worker struggles to keep his faith, to "live as Jesus did, at least some of the time," while the rest of the time accommodating to his situation in a neighborhood, a nation, he is, with respect to such efforts, not unlike that only pope who ever quit his job: Celestino V left the Vatican to return to his hermit's life as a monk (and, soon thereafter, die). "I win, I lose," that factory worker acknowledges with a shrug, and with no claim to originality in the use of those four words, even as one suspects that the weary pope of the thirteenth century had a similar line of reasoning cross his mind as he departed the big city for the sanctuary (the sanctity) of the countryside.

It is no accident that the central character in Silone's *Bread and Wine*, Pietro Spina, is named after the Pietro da Morrone who became briefly the pope. In the novel Pietro Spina is a revolutionary on the run, hiding in the garb of a priest. The novel, in fact, renders brilliantly and affectingly the mix of idealism and pragmatism that even a principled warrior in the fight for social change must summon in his daily life. Irony abounds in the story: the hero's soulful decency, no matter that he is a hunted man, declared a criminal by the state; indeed, his sanctity, no matter his full commitment to the secular—he is an ardent socialist who wants a better world for humble workers, near penniless farmers. Pietro is hiding when he dresses as a priest, but the reader readily realizes that all too many "real" priests lack the impressive spiritual qualities Silone has given his protagonist. An utterly secular materialist bears himself nobly, earns his right to a Roman collar so often betrayed in history, as Pope Celestino knew, and as Silone first came to know as a fifteen-year-old lad, when a severe earthquake did terrible damage to Italy's Abruzzo region where he lived, the son of a peasant. In a mere eight seconds fifty thousand people were killed, and thousands more, already poor, were reduced to even further vulnerability. Under such circumstances the local bishop and his entourage promptly fled to safer territory, a secular journey, and the young boy, Tranquilli Secondo (Ignazio Silone is a pseudonym), watched that departure with surprise, consternation, disgust. Here, he knew, was a kind of lived secularism; here, as Dorothy Day once put it, was "Christ betrayed—as He has been again and again by clergymen, never mind those who attack and denounce the Church." She loved *Bread and Wine* for precisely that reason: its willingness to confound anyone looking for a clear-cut sorting of people, believers as against nonbelievers. Silone confounds, thereby, the sacred and the secular, wants us to remember the spirituality of the doubter, the crass self-interest of many who wrap themselves in the paraphernalia and claims of religious affiliation.

Once in a discussion with Dorothy Day about the very subject matter of this section of the book, the way secularism has manifested itself at various moments in religious history, she begged to disagree with my notion, then, that only recently has the secular achieved the prominence we take for granted today: "I think you underestimate *doubt* as a constant part of faith—in any century; and I think you are making too much of science (and social science) as the (recent) 'causes' of secularism. I don't deny that today there is the authority of scientific knowledge to elicit or encourage or give a kind of *imprimatur* to secularism; but for Heaven's sake, the secular world has always been 'there,' or 'here'—that's the big story of the Old Testament and the New Testament, and it's the big story, sad to say, of Christianity, both Catholicism and Protestantism. You've been talking [I had, alas] as if Galileo and Newton and Einstein and Freud have been the 'big guns' that have been shooting down religious faith, religious ties in people (in the West). To me, those folks and the people who follow their lead are part of a much longer story, and I wonder sometimes whether it isn't our conceit to think of ourselves as all that different.

"Before there were microscopes and telescopes and psychoanalysts and physicists, there were *cardinals*, there were Lutheran *bishops* who loved to 'live it up,' who had a great time for themselves, and who, I suspect, had less spirituality in them than—Einstein, who, at least, wondered about the mystery of the world and was humbled by it, all that mystery. Oh, I know—you can define 'secular' in several ways, and I suppose the same goes for 'spiritual.' I suppose that if you say that a society is 'secular,' because it's not under the authority of a church, the major influence of a church—then more societies in Europe are now secular than [was the case] in 1400 and 1500. But I'm trying to follow Saint Paul when he said 'not the letter, but the spirit,' which was what Jesus kept emphasizing, and so if the society *isn't* 'secular' because a church runs its schools and the politicians have to check things out with the people in that church, and the newspapers have to be careful in the same way—yes, that's a 'religious' nation, in a certain way, or a 'nonsecular' one, and the children growing up there may be more influenced by church doctrine as it's transmitted in classrooms. But that's only a part of the story: you can have religion betrayed from within—it happens all the time. God had a long, hard time with His chosen people, the Jews, persuading them to live in accordance with His principles, and Jesus has been betrayed over and over again by every kind of Christian church there is. I'll never forget Jacques Maritain [the Catholic theologian] telling me, 'Dorothy, I worry more about the harm done to "The Mystical Body of Jesus" by those of us who claim to be devout Catholics than by the agnostic scientists and the people who believe in them.' I wasn't sure what he was getting at then, but he tried to explain it all to me, as I'm trying to [do so] now to you! I guess I want to cast a wider net with that word 'secular,' and I want to be careful that we don't let the words 'sacred' or 're-ligious'—the opposite of secular—go unexamined!"

No question, historically words such as "secular" or "secularism" or "secularization" bespoke shifts in the way people thought and acted, in the way their children were educated, in the way even property was distributed and managed:a shift from ecclesiastical power, as it was variously wielded, to what became known as temporal or civil or lay control. In a philosophical sense secular-ism also referred to the well-being of people while they lived here on this earth—as opposed to a concern for them in a supposed future state, when they would fall under the Lord's rule. But in the past, as now, how all those matters of property and politics and power and ideology, as it had access to people through words, cere-monies, mandates backed by military force, got worked into the individual minds of various men, women, chil-dren (and yes, into the minds of ecclesiastical officials, or civil leaders) would yield only to a kind of scrutiny obviously unavailable to us: those hours of inquiry that get called an interview, a recorded discussion shaped by direct questions aimed at illuminating how a "culture" settles into a particular person's thoughts, memories, as-pirations, worries, inclinations.

To be sure, the degree of *formal* secularization has ob-viously shifted over the centuries. The United States it-self is a nation explicitly founded by people who chafed under one or another kind of ecclesiastical authority: we are, it can be said, the first modern nation founded as explicitly secularist—that is, in response to societies where secularism was one of a number of competing ways of thinking. God figures in our important early political documents, but so does a temporal or civic reasoning that clearly has first legal place in our country's scheme of things. Collectively, therefore, we became, at the start, a secular nation; yet, of course, the many communities within our borders have had their own values, faiths. They were even "free" to do so in the midst of a kind of racial servitude just short of slavery as recently as 1963, so I was told, that year, in Greenwood, Mississippi, by a black woman who had her own way of talking about "secularism" in America now, or in America "back then" when her people first lived here: "I've often wondered what crossed their minds—when they just arrived to be at the mercy of all those bossmen. Who will ever know? We sure did 'take' to Jesus, though! Lord knows what our folks in Africa believed, but after we got here we got the God we know now—and there will be moments when I wonder what He thinks of all this, what's happened to us [African-American] people. Everyone talks about how you should believe this and you should believe that, and never let go of God no matter how high and mighty you become. (No worry that we're in danger of *that* happening!) But I will wonder the reverse—what He be thinking of those high and mighty folks who sit in those churches telling Him to look after them, because they're so good.

"You know what? My family hasn't ever stopped praying to God; we do it all the time, before and after we eat, and on getting up and going to sleep, all like that. We try to be God-fearing, that's one thing you can do here, no matter the bad condition we're in! We're God-fearing people, even if the whites call us those terrible names. Maybe God knows all this, what's happened in the past, and what's happening now, and so he's just waiting to pass His judgments—to say y'all colored, you've been the believers, and y'all whites, you've been the heathen folk! [It] goes to show you, what seems to be, may not be, and what God will favor and call His own is His business and will come out when He's ready, and it won't be hereabouts in Mississippi where He'll make His announcements of who's with Him, and who's against Him."

Although one might conclude that she is not being especially original—that she is speaking the received pieties of a family's life—in fact she had delivered a lecture on the difficulties that confront an observer, however learned theologically, who attempts to decide how to recognize secularism. The white folks she knew so well (whom I also got to know and interview) were at pains to express their dissatisfaction with what some of them (a minister, a school official, a lawyer) kept calling "America's secular culture." What they posed as a desirable alternative was a "Christian culture, like we once had here, before television and the movies made things bad even in our neck of the woods," so the lawyer put it. When I told my black informant what that prominent attorney had told me, she laughed heartily, said she would be praying for him, then offered this observation: "They can call themselves all they want, but (you know what?) they're in a huge lot of trouble, because it's

God who calls the shots on what they are, who they be, and so their words are just a lot of air that comes out of their big-shot mouths. I do believe they're making a mistake counting on Him as the one who'll back them up in their opinion of themselves."

Those last words rang in my ears years afterwards. I remembered them especially in 1990 at a conference at Harvard Divinity School when I kept hearing talk of "secular America" and our "secular society," and the "Christian Coalition" as it was "resisting secularism." As George Orwell reminded us, words can be used as property—and thereby we who use them can become the blind leading the blind. Secularism may be a matter of property owned, school curricula shaped in a certain direction, a culture transmitted along certain lines; but if the ultimate criterion is the relationship between all of that and *God's* judgment (rather than our judgment of His judgment), then we'd best, as that black woman suggested, take due care and pause: hedge carefully not only our personal bets (if such a wager even interests us) but also our categorical ones through which we come down this way, that way, with respect to the sacred, the profane, the religiously connected, the secularly disposed.

II

Where We Stood

1900

HISTORICAL ironies ought to give us cautionary pause as we contemplate secularism, yet cultural shifts obviously do take place over time, even if they prompt paradoxical consequences—a burst of "enlightenment" stirring an outburst of reactive nostalgia, if not a reactionary revulsion, a turn toward what was as a bulwark against what threatens to be. To contemplate a thoroughly secular Vatican, in the Middle Ages, at the height of its power across the European nations, to contemplate a slave or sharecropper population humbly, passionately, often furtively tied to the sacred, amidst a privileged, materialist white world that not rarely insisted upon turning its churchgoing into a weekly episode of self-display, is to be mindful of what William Carlos Williams, thinking about America's evolution from the seventeenth to the twentieth century, called "the zig and the zag of things," an earthy poet, through vernacular expression, bringing the Hegelian dialectic to his native New Jersey as he readied himself for the writing of his great poem *Paterson*. Individual minds vary in response to political or social changes, intellectual shifts in opinion, but those changes prompt all sorts of people to stop and think about what they believe and why, hence the accentuations of the secular or, on the contrary, the reactive flight from it.

Certainly, the second half of the nineteenth century had a decisive impact on the secularist assumptions in the West, to the point that if one wants to talk of a modern secular mind, its immediate and persuasive antecedents had come into being by the last years of the nineteenth century, the first ones of the twentieth century. It is well to remember that in 1880 Darwin, Freud, Marx, and Einstein were all alive, as were George Eliot, Hardy, Tolstoy, Dostoievsky: the giant minds of the sciences and social science that have shaped our time, and, too, the giant novelists who had examined in their different ways the secular manner of thinking that nourished the breakthrough of *An Origin of Species by Means of Natural Selection* or *The Preservation of Favoured Races in the Struggle for Life* (both 1859), or *Das Kapital* (1867), or *The Interpretation of Dreams* (1900), or the seminal four papers on theoretical physics in which the theory of relativity was proposed (1905). Darwin's work, in particular, radically unnerved thousands who held a biblical view of humankind's historical story; and to this day the implications of his thinking for biology (and even psychology and sociology) have been profound. He himself became an agnostic and saw no great overall moral or philosophical meaning in the long chronology of our being, which he regarded, rather, as a story of accidents and incidents, of chance and circumstance as they all came to bear on "natural selection." Although Copernicus and Galileo and Newton have been absorbed, so to speak, by traditional Christianity, by no means has Darwin's view of our origin and destiny been universally integrated into the teachings, the theology, of many religions that rely upon the Bible for their inspiration, their sense of who we are, where we came from, how our purpose here ought to be described. It was one thing for scientists to probe the planets, declare that this place we inhabit is only one spot in a seemingly endless number of places in an ever expanding universe, or to examine closely our body's cells, or those of other creatures; it was quite another matter to suggest that we ourselves are merely an aspect of an ever changing nature, that our "origin" was not "divine" but a consequence of a biological saga of sorts.

Meanwhile, in the Vienna of the 1890s, a young neurologist and psychiatrist was examining the mind in the way Darwin had examined the physical side of our being. Freud didn't take our thoughts at face value, any more than Darwin took at face value our present bodily nature. Freud, too, was interested in "evolution," in the way ideas and desires and habits and preferences develop in the course of their own kind of "struggle for life." He dared call upon himself, his dreams, his passing thoughts, the jokes he'd heard, remembered, told others, the turns and twists of his mind's life—and so doing, he assumed that to a degree the universal might be known through the particular with regard to the most private part of ourselves, the emotions we feel by day and, he emphasized, while asleep. Such a line of inquiry, of reasoning, had implications for psychiatry, of course, but as W. H. Auden famously noted in his memorial poem to Freud, psychoanalytic theory became "a whole climate of opinion," and as a consequence secularism gained a new hold on what once had been the prerogative of the sacred. In the Old Testament it is God who knows man, Who sees through him in his manipulative greed, in his puny, ill-fated attempts to pull this or that fast one, circumvent set religious bounds. It is God who punishes, but it is also God who listens, who interprets, who heals, especially in the New Testament, when He became man: Jesus the ever understanding one who has an eye for the troubled in spirit and, invariably, a story that helps explain what is happening, puts things in a larger (human, moral) perspective. Moreover, the institutionalization of Christ's teaching and healing ministry in the form of a Church enabled priests not only to say Mass but to attend parishioners, hear them out, marry them, baptize their children, see them through death, and, more personally, listen to their confessions, week after week.

Now, a physician was telling the world, in the first years of a new century, that he and his colleagues in Vienna, in Budapest, in Berlin knew about what was *really* being conveyed in those confessions—and in many other expressive moments hitherto the psychological domain of the clergy and, by extension, of the Lord. Today, we take for granted "pastoral counseling," but we may not realize what a displacement of sorts psychoanalysis caused when it became, increasingly, the cultural authority with respect to our mental life. A public surrender began to take place almost immediately upon the publication of Freud's first book, a rising acknowledgment that his kind of knowledge commanded not only surprise, attention, but also the respect, grudging in many instances, that goes with a physician's, a scientist's, explanations. The heated denunciations of psychoanalysis and its founder on the part of the clergy were, needless to say, both noteworthy and instructive. It is hard for some of us, at the end of this century, to realize the intensity of clerical opposition visited upon that small band of psychological investigators who lived in Central Europe. In conversations with Anna Freud I heard echoes of the harsh noise she quite clearly remembered to the end of her life: "I was a teenager when my father began to be—'notorious' might be an appropriate word, I fear. [She was born in 1895.] I recall my father talking with my brothers. They were hearing from their friends that he was controversial, that he was saying things that weren't 'right.' It was hard for all of us to know what we should do—I think that word 'right' was being used in a judgmental way, a morally condemning way, rather than as a 'scientific evaluation.' I know my father worried about the Catholic Church— it was a real 'power,' then, in the [Austro-Hungarian] empire, and it was no fun, as some of the children say these days, to incur the displeasure of priests and bishops! And we did [hear or read of that displeasure]—I can remember my father saying out loud some of what was written: they called psychoanalysis 'godless.' He nodded when he read that [allegation]—but he wasn't smiling. He was worried—though he never let his concerns hold him back from giving expression to what he believed: one way or another he got his ideas across, on paper, or in conversations. I do remember him saying this: 'They are right, psychoanalysis *is* 'godless,' it *is* 'godless materialism.'

"You know, it was his job, from the start, to understand how we behave, the reasons for the emotions we experience. He was a scientist, and he was trying to do research in an 'area' that was off-limits, you could say. It was priests who were supposed to deal with psychology, not doctors. Yes, it is true, traditional university psychology didn't stir the alarm and antagonism that came to us [I had suggested as much]. The reason was that we were much 'broader' in our outlook—we weren't studying 'reflexes' in animals or in people; we were talking about the emotions of all people, and about the conscience, and about the secrets people carry in them and inadvertently express, or reveal indirectly. This had always been the territory of religion—the priest had access to the fears and worries of his parishioners; and he was told by them of the mistakes they made, the wrongs they'd done. The priest had his confessional booth, and there my father was, with his consulting room, and his couch—this was an 'infringement,' some people called it, and it was turning 'spirit' into 'flesh,' making the spiritual a matter of mere events in the mind, each of which carried an explanation, if you looked closely and long enough."

A pause, and an unusual physical display of emotion, a vigorous shaking of the head, meant to convey the long past heat of those days, the bitterness of the accusations as they were leveled at a time and in a national and cultural setting altogether different from the one in which she and I (at Yale University in 1972) then found ourselves. But I also realized that the movement of her head was meant to convey to me a glimpse of the naysaying she had just recollected, tried to evoke for me descriptively. She herself promptly realized as much: "I think my father had a high tolerance for anxiety and fear! He was called a lot of names, but somehow he kept his wits about him, and also kept saying and writing what he believed to be true. I suspect that the reason he caused such a storm was that he was a clearheaded writer, whose ideas got across to the general public. If he'd buried them, all his thoughts, in obscure medical journals, far fewer people would have been aroused to anger. But he became a well-known writer, and *there* he was twice a trespasser—daring to step into what priests believed to be their territory, and daring to address some of their parishioners, you could say, [meaning] the men and women who bought books."

Another pause, and then a brief acknowledgment of a kind: "I suppose those who called his work 'godless' were picking up not only what he said, but his own personal beliefs. I think it's only fair to say that if 'we' can respond unconsciously to others, they in turn can do so with us! But I am repeating myself here; I am saying that it was not only what my father said, but how he said it, and where he said it. He could be blunt, and he wanted his ideas to be known outside of the universities. Anyway, he was never welcomed, in those early years, in the universities. Even late in his life, he wasn't welcomed in many of them—I know that well: after the [Second World] War, I received invitations every day, it seemed, to come and receive honorary degrees or medals or scrolls of recognition and gratitude. They were all belatedly meant for him! Finally, his work was being accepted, at least in some quarters—much less so in academic psychology and psychiatry than among people who represented the humanities, interestingly enough, and not at all, still, in some important religious circles. Even now, there is much opposition to psychoanalysis—many want to pick and choose what [of it] they like and feel free to use, as against what they have no intention of accepting, in fact, keep calling a threat to their religious beliefs or their moral principles."

With some trepidation I raised with her the matter of Freud's book *The Future of an Illusion*, a resolutely critical analysis of religious faith; it compares faith to infantile neuroses, wherein children develop fantasies for various reasons, cling to them tenaciously as if they were facts. The tone of the book is uncharacteristically harsh, even scornful, not the way Freud usually addressed readers, and the book lacks the wide range of subject matter he studied and then described for others in his elegantly written essays. Miss Freud, usually quite willing to explore whatever topic I brought up, certainly including her father's many books and articles, was herself uncharacteristically terse and, I thought, toughly dismissive of those who have had reservations about that book. She also pointedly stopped referring to her "father" and instead called him several times "Freud" (prompting me to feel that the full weight of his magisterial career was being summoned): "When Freud decided to deal directly with the question of religion, he knew he was asking for trouble. This is an almost universal matter [religious belief], and it won't yield easily (if at all!) to reason. *That* is what he meant when he spoke of infantile neurosis—he wasn't accusing anyone, so much as acknowledging what had transpired. As you know, to speak of 'infantile neurosis' in connection with anyone is to describe them as a fellow human being!"

Abrupt, flat silence—I am surprised, feel myself arraigned, lose my nerve, abandon this direction of the conversation, and quickly steer us to something far more agreeable to Miss Freud and, by then, to me: her work, at one time, with certain law professors at Yale Law School. Days later, I pick up my copy of *The Future of an Illusion*. I find it marked throughout with my responsive pencil marks, as in this section at the end of chapter 6, when Freud establishes an imaginary dialogue in order to further his point of view:

> Well then, if even obdurate skeptics admit that the assertions of religion cannot be refuted by reason, why should I not believe in them, since they have so much on their side—tradition, the agreement of mankind, and all the consolations they offer? Why not, indeed! Just as no one can be forced to believe, so no one can be forced to disbelieve. But do not let us be satisfied with deceiving ourselves that arguments like these take us along the road of correct thinking. If ever there was a case of a lame excuse we have it here. Ignorance is ignorance; no right to believe anything can be derived from it. In other matters no sensible person will behave so irresponsibly or rest content with such feeble grounds for his opinions and for the line he takes.

I read passages such as that carefully, conclude yet again that their tone is unlike what I have welcomed when in the midst of other books by the same author. I try to put myself (for a second or two, and I hope and pray with due modesty) in Freud's shoes—why such an abrupt dismissal of a subject much more complicated than he is willing to let it be? I think of Saint Augustine and of Kierkegaard and of twentieth-century individuals I've known or whose work I've studied, such as Reinhold Niebuhr, and Dietrich Bonhoeffer, and Dorothy

Day, and I find Freud's version of their interests and convictions inadequate, to say the least. Indeed, I find his approach to religion all too instructive about himself and thoroughly ironic, given the creedal nature of institutional psychoanalysis, the splits and fiercely fought disagreements, and the reverential attitude of certain psychoanalysts toward the founding father, as in Hans Sachs's book, titled *Freud: Master and Friend.* Anna Freud said as much on repeated occasions when speaking at particular psychoanalytic institutes, not quite in the way I just have, but with no wish, either, to hide her sense of things: the rigidity of belief that for a while had seized many in this new, quite prominent and influential occupation. In his epilogue to *Childhood and Society* one of my teachers, Erik H. Erikson, referred to the "talmudic orthodoxy" that he felt had descended on all too many analysts, and the analyst Allen Wheelis addressed the same matter on a number of occasions, and most especially in *The Quest for Identity.*

I bring all this up because Freud's attitude toward religion became itself an article of belief for many in my field and very much gave a particular shape to certain strains of secularism in the twentieth century almost from the start. To call upon Erikson, whose work on both Luther and Gandhi demonstrated that psychoanalytic inquiry needn't take the direction Freud pursued: "When I go back to the 1920s, I realize that those of us in [psychoanalytic] training then were declared agnostics or atheists, or if we had a religious side to us, we kept it out of anyone's hearing. Some of our teachers were already becoming oracular figures, and not just for us [students]. They were quick to point out the opposition to themselves and their ideas on the part of the Catholic Church, or the Lutheran Church in Germany; but they weren't as willing to examine their own way of looking at religious and spiritual matters—this [attitude] from people who claimed to be endlessly engaged in 'self-analysis' as well as the work they did with their analysands. What these leaders [in psychoanalysis] believed, their followers [younger analysts] also believed—and it went much further, because psychoanalysis started having an enormous impact on all sorts of important and well-to-do people, the ones who knew about it, and could afford it, and by that I mean not only that they had the money to pay for daily sessions, but they also had the time, lots of time, that it takes to have such an experience. I can see why many religious people didn't find their way to psychoanalysis at first—its assumptions weren't congenial to them. But in time its assumptions became part of—so much: the intellectual world, the movies and the theater, the world of artists and writers and journalists, and, in America especially, the psychiatric and medical world. In time, that secular world of the Western democracies was very much under the spell of what used to be called 'Freudian thought'—that phrase became an increasingly noticeable mantra!"

Needless to say, Freud's manner of approach to spirituality, to religious commitment was singularly blunt, unqualified, dismissive, and, many would argue, unknowing in its refusal even to examine a complex reflective response to our human situation with a subtlety, a nuance worthy of his own willingness in other instances to demonstrate a tentativeness in keeping with the many-sided nature of what he was trying to understand. When William James examined religion in *The Varieties of Religious Experience*, he was careful to be inquiring, descriptive, rather than the scornful critic for whom psychology has become yet another weapon of confrontation, refutation. Put differently, James wrote in the tradition of European phenomenology, wherein our actions are regarded closely, conveyed to others in a language meant to render them justly, with a full appreciation of any ironies and contradictions observed. Freud, on the other hand, was predominantly analytic in his sensibility, as the name he gave to his profession certainly indicates—moreover, he was, by his own description, a conquistador, meaning a fighter who proposed to win at all costs. In the tradition of self-assured noblesse oblige, James tried constantly to be generous to those with whom he did not necessarily see eye to eye; Freud, in contrast, felt very much at the margins of a world closely connected to powerful religious institutions that saw his work (apart from his explicit writing on the subject of spiritual faith) as threatening, indeed. In 1906 James heard Freud speak in the course of his only American visit, told him that the future was his, a salutation, even an act of reverence, one cannot quite imagine being offered by Freud to another important psychological observer. When Freud was ready to acknowledge his admiration, he used the image of military struggle (in keeping, I suppose, with his notion of himself as one at constant war with various opponents: ignorance, true, but also other individuals who have claimed to know about our lives, our aspirations and concerns). In his essay "Dostoievski and Parricide" he begins by calling *The Brothers Karamazov* "the most magnificent novel ever written," declares "the episode of the Grand Inquisitor one of the peaks in the literature of the world," and then this: "Before the problem of the creative artist analysis must, alas, lay down its arms." Were he himself examining such a train of thinking, he might raise an eyebrow, wonder why an enormous achievement, an unparalleled success, need be turned into a "problem"—one not yet conquered by weaponry. But his essential realization (that novelists have, as it were, quietly, unpretentiously been there even before he and his kind arrived, claiming victory in the name of science) certainly is borne out in the oeuvre of Dostoievsky (whose Grand Inquisitor argument, in its mix of grace and agility and powerful persuasion, seems to have taught the admiring Freud very little when he sat down to write *The Future of an Illusion*); that realization is also supported by the work of several other nineteenth-century novelists, whose psychological awareness, and refinement of perception, and whose way of giving expression to the range of our human inwardness makes so very much of contemporary social science research and writing pale badly in comparison.

In fact, George Eliot, all through *Middlemarch* (1872), more than anticipates Freud: she relentlessly examines the unconscious, uses several of her characters to do so, and, too, clearly indicates an acute sense of what Freud only later in his richly productive career knew to call "ego psychology": the way we come to terms with the unconscious through various mental maneuvers. Moreover, she did not isolate psychology from sociology or, for that matter, politics. The central figure in the novel is, really, the town itself, its stubbornly held customs, values, but also the changes that gradually come to bear on it. The various characters in this carefully plotted story, so richly endowed with social and psychological wisdom, are meant to embody the full range of a particular, historical moment and scene—the rural England of the earlier part of the nineteenth century. But, naturally, Eliot wants us to move beyond that world, however fine and telling her evocation of it; she is in pursuit of moral knowledge of a kind that, she hopes, transcends the limits of time and place.

The author of *Scenes of a Clerical Life* summoned occasional, guarded irony for her social descriptions in that respectful group portrait of ministers and their parishioners; but *Middlemarch* is a secular story, and its church life, such as it is, offers a mere nod to ceremonial commemoration. True, at certain moments Eliot tips her hand as the onetime earnest student of religious philosophy, who actually intended, as a young woman, to write an ecclesiastical history of England. She brings us to a church; she gives us a clergyman—but through him we learn of the fast slipping hold of religious conviction on these essentially secular folk, each earnestly or warily or cleverly or mischievously trying to make do, if not make off with any and all good fortune available. At times, actually, she is more scornful, as a social critic, than Freud would dare be: a striking departure for this daughter of Robert Evans, a loyal member of the Anglican Church and the manager of a country estate, whom she, in her last, autobiographical writing, described as a country parson. Here in book 4 of *Middlemarch* is biblical life under a psychological lens that is sardonically secular: "When the animals entered the Ark in pairs, one may imagine that allied species made much private remark on one another, and were tempted to think that so many forms feeding on the same store of fodder were eminently superfluous, as tending to diminish the rations (I fear the part played by the vultures on that occasion would be too painful for art to represent, those birds being disadvantageously naked about the gullet, and apparently without rites and ceremonies)."

As if the above were not enough, the authorial voice escalates its scorn, makes a damaging connection between the far-distant past and the nineteenth-century English country scene being evoked: "The same sort of temptation befell the Christian Carnivora who formed Peter Featherstone's funeral procession; most of them having their minds bent on a limited store which each would have liked to get the most of." She quite obviously need not have used that capitalized phrase to accomplish her comparative assertion. When Dorothea, rather than the novelist directly, is speaking, we learn more gently, even wistfully, of a falling away from religion on the part of a central character in the story, an ardent idealist who first marries a biblical scholar, as a matter of fact, the older, desiccated Casaubon. At one point Dorothea tells Will Ladislaw, "I have always been finding out my religion since I was a little girl"; but she is quick to point out what has now transpired: "I used to pray so much—now I hardly ever pray."

Dorothea is not George Eliot, but neither is she unlike her in important respects—a strong intellectuality, an articulate reformist spirit, a shrewd sense of others (which does not necessarily translate into a firm grasp of one's own inner nature). Young Mary Ann Evans was a devoutly introspective Christian lady who read far and deep in not only the Bible but any number of theological sources. It took her several decades of secular London living to shed that background, and in a sense her novel *Middlemarch* tells of that transformation: a personal one that mirrored the emerging secularism of certain sophisticated precincts of nineteenth-century London. In those paragraphs above, psychological skepticism becomes an instrument of probing social analysis, which is, in turn, trumped by a contemptuously bitter designation ("Christian Carnivora") that arguably gives a clue to a writer's temporary lack of personal control. She has already more than made her point and will have plenty of opportunity to continue to develop the notion of greed as the triumphant survivor of death, and, too, of such covetousness as is ironically and routinely wrapped in the clothes of Christian worship. Yet she has to summon a biological word, "Carnivora," to seal the matter in the reader's mind—as if she has lost confidence in her own narrative ability to encompass the state of affairs at hand: the joining of public sorrow, traditionally expressed in a church, and private cupidity, not rare even in brilliant, well-educated agnostics, who surely have their particular rituals and protocols and observances to endure, while they harbor their own lustfully acquisitive daydreams, fancies.

Freud's "analysis" of the psychological sources of religious faith would strike his friendly critics as a natural outcome of a combatively argumentative, agnostic essayist's desire to strike yet another blow for Intellect or Reason over what he regarded as the murkier recesses of our irrational life, where what we want is so often confused with what is or ought to be. George Eliot's portrayal of the mind (as opposed to her occasional social outbursts) is as layered, textured as Freud's psychological writing at its best; she is not propounding ideology but, rather, telling a story that allows her leeway to discuss the biggest of topics through the indirection of human relatedness as it can be rendered in all its ambiguities and inconsistencies and outright contradictions through the construction of characters and a plot in which their thoughts and actions unfold. Even as Eliot looked back in *Middlemarch* to the Age of Reform, the earlier decades of the nineteenth century, when suffrage gradually became available to more and more individuals in both rural and urban England, she also was looking ahead to the consequences of the political and cultural changes she was bringing to life in this most ambitious of her novels. In a sense, she is taking the measure of a world becoming more conclusively secular— where once great and constant consideration was given to the "image of God," now the mind of man commanded the major attention of people who may have attended church regularly, but who looked less upward toward the heavens than directly in a nearby mirror.

In the phrase "unreflecting egoism" Eliot captures the breadth and depth of such secular preoccupation. She was, of course, decades ahead of Freud, in her acknowledgment, that way, of the unconscious, its raw power constantly assertive, no matter our notion of ourselves as in (conscious) control of what we say or do. Her portraits in *Middlemarch* are unsparing in their insistence that appearances, even those that are connected to

church attendance or high-minded acts of social gener-
osity, don't tell the whole story of individuals or of
groups of men and women. Faith is the continual subject of her close scrutiny: the sometimes insincere faith
in God of those ministers who claim to act in His name,
but also the faltering faith of ordinary people; and too,
other kinds of faith, such as that we place in certain
professions (medicine) or institutions (the universities).
Interestingly, she reserves for a businessman, a banker,
Bulstrode, the most strenuous and affecting of spiritual
struggles. As for her physician, Dr. Lydgate, he soon
enough loses his high ideals to the demands of an all too
shallow, self-regarding wife—and does so without so
much as a moral blink. He simply settles down, accom-
modates himself to a particular marriage: "He had
gained an excellent practice, alternating, according to
the season, between London and a Continental bath-
ing-place, having written a thesis on Gout, a disease
which has a great deal of wealth on its side." Eliot portrays such an outcome, such an obvious moral decline,
not as a tragedy and, surely, not as a sin (a shortcoming
that is spiritual in nature), but as the mere manifes-
tation of a powerfully determining psychology that decisively shapes the outcome of lives. At one point she
circles around the ever present riddle of will, its relationship to social fate: "It always remains true that if we
had been greater, circumstances would have been less
strong against us." At another point, less speculative or
philosophical, she settles for a humdrum marital scene
all too worthy of the television talk shows, the self-help
books, which a century later would give us not quite the

level of access to the life of our Dr. Lydgates and our Rosamonds (his wife) that this analysis does: "Between him and her indeed there was that total missing of each other's mental track, which is too evidently possible even between persons who are continually thinking of each other."

Such a comment is not handed down in an oracular manner (as is sometimes the case in this novel more than any of her others) but is, rather, immersed in a rather casual yet careful and precise description of the way a particular couple gets along. What matters in life, we are persuaded, what gives it direction and character, has to do with how we get along with one another: one person's interests and dispositions as they connect with another person's. Our young physician is not a "good" person come to naught by virtue of a "bad" marriage; nor is the woman he chooses to marry the bearer of evil, someone who corrupts a person otherwise intended for idealism (in the mind of the author, the reader). We have, here, gone (as the saying would have us think) "beyond good and evil," be it in the biblical sense or in the somewhat alternative sense of human reflection with respect to right and wrong (theology, moral philosophy). Now it is the accidents of our various encounters and, thereafter, the implications of "interpersonal psychology" that in their sum have the final say on who and what we become.

By the same token, Dorothea Brooke and her husband Casaubon turn out to be an ironic prelude (despite all their high-and-mighty ideas, aims) to today's thoroughly commonplace "dysfunctional" marriages.

Eliot is devastating in her controlled satire as she develops that "relationship," as we know to call it. She causes us, initially, to be much taken with Dorothea, who in certain respects seems no less than an authorial stand-in; yet gradually we begin to see that a very bright and deep-thinking and far-reaching mind can also be a dim-witted one emotionally, maybe even morally. If Casaubon is meant to represent a sterile, a badly compromised and weakened religious and theological tradition, Dorothea's choice of him (her capacity to build him up, for a while, in her mind as someone he isn't) is surely intended to remind us that visions are constructed not only in the name of God but out of our ordinary human frailty. And no amount of education or intellectual brilliance will banish that frailty, hence psychology as the great leveling presence among us all.

In the first pages of *Middlemarch* Eliot shrewdly plays on the moral, if not spiritual, yearnings of her readers, not to mention of her own life as a keenly reformist observer of nineteenth-century Victorian society. We take to Dorothea immediately and compare her, with knowing favor, to her sister Celia, who seems a conventional person of no great thought, of no subtle feeling. Yet, gradually, Celia's common sense and unselfconscious decency, her seemingly "simple" life such a contrast to the pain and strain of Dorothea's introspection, begin to win us over, even as Dorothea emerges as someone too clever by half, as far less discerning in things that really count (how you live your life, with whom)—as opposed to the matters that her advanced intellect is always pondering. Eliot is comparing the old-fashioned natural piety of an earlier time (Celia) with a new kind of cultural and psychological awareness, proudly distanced from the traditional supports of church and social status. Whereas Celia will soon enough be integrated into a life as a wife, a mother, a well-to-do member of a country scene, a churchgoer, Dorothea wants to change the world and looks askance at many of its claims; hence her constantly skeptical mind that, her creator lets us know, can turn unwittingly arrogant. That is the nub of the difference, we begin to realize, between these two sisters: the ready acceptance of the past, as it has handed down its requirements, on the part of Celia, as against Dorothea's quick suspicion of so very much in that past. The latter becomes in many respects a modern person, very much on her own, sometimes to the benefit of certain people (when her intensely charitable nature seeks expression), but sometimes to her own detriment, not to mention that of others (when she swallows whole all kinds of untested new ideas, or treats those she regards as "slow" or "selfish" or hopelessly tied to the customary, the ordinary, in an instructively patronizing or dismissive fashion).

It is, finally, the customary, and the ordinary, even the lowly, who emerge from this novel with our highest regard—perhaps because they receive less attention than their "betters," and because the author has reluctantly come to realize that while her more privileged characters go about their willful and sometimes mistaken ways, these "rustics," such as Timothy Cooper, comparatively minor figures in a novel's large scheme of things, maintain their solid hold on the world's daily rhythms, enabled in their exertions not by fancy theories or highly touted new proposals but "through a hard process of feeling" that is, in turn, the result of dawn-to-dusk labor, year in and year out. "Timothy was a wiry old labourer," we are told, and he mouths a kind of refractory and earthy populism that won't yield to what is being offered in the name of secular "enlightenment," "progress," "reform." We learn through his brief appearance how easy it is to overlook people like him, or to assume the right to speak for him, or to mistake the nature of his moral bearings. He seems to resist not only the idea of progress but its specifics, such as the railroad. In fact, however, he takes the shrewd measure of what others too quickly find congenial, welcome. Whereas those with new secular ideas, in the name of politics or economics or out of "a neatly carved argument for a social benefit," urge one or another departure from what was in favor of a quite different destination, a Timothy Cooper can make quite clear his practical or moral reservations. We learn, in *Middlemarch*, how little notice, never mind admiration, he and those like him are getting, amidst the acceleration of industrial and ideological change in nineteenth-century capitalist England, even its rural precincts. Nor is the issue only one of class. Eliot is at pains to remind us that the well-to-do can join with the humble in a shrewd hesitation to embrace certain new customs and beliefs, even as both the poor and the rich can come together in an effort to break with the past, accept with satisfaction—indeed, pride—what is unprecedented, yet so promising, inviting.

Throughout the novel the old Judeo-Christian notion of "pride" as a grave instance of moral failure struggles with a new notion of pride as a necessary affirmation of one's human inclination to build, to make the
world anew. Again, with irony, the most old-fashioned
and intense, even Augustinian, self-scrutiny, is granted
to Bulstrode, a character whom another author (Dickens, perhaps) might have been tempted to caricature—
and Eliot herself may have been initially so inclined.
Certainly he is not an attractive figure at any point in
the story, and Eliot moves cautiously to unnerve us
through her presentation of his moral struggle. In the
beginning he is yet another ambitious social upstart
on the make: he gets called, for instance, "suave." We
are happily immersed in Dr. Lydgate's moral crisis, in
that of Dorothea; yet the very idea of Bulstrode's having
such a conflict seems well beyond him and, as well, his
creator, whose personal life seemed to prepare her well
for the making of characters whose evident secular
"goodness" has to be tested in various ways. In Bulstrode, however, she shows herself prepared to take a
second and more charitable (maybe "thoughtful" is
the required descriptive word here) look at the nature of
religious introspection: a smooth, canny, manipulative
banker, with a past he wants hidden, turns out to be,
however fleetingly, a sinner sweating out not only his
secular fears but his moral jeopardy. By no means,
though, does he ever become a spiritually redeemed
person. He wants the dissolute Raffles out of the way
lest he reveal what he knows, plenty damaging to a
banker who has tried hard and with considerable success to achieve not only the power that accompanies the

control of money, but a more elusive yet quite satisfying respectability: the neighborly nods of approval that count a lot during a day spent out in the world.

This episode allows Eliot to cut deep to the bone of a society fast changing from a mostly village one, bound together by values rooted in agricultural life, and by an unquestioned ecclesiastical authority—wielded constantly as an aspect of everyday existence, from baptisms to marriages to deathbed prayers and funerals—to a commercial world in which individuals rather than institutions have the predominant say: the entrepreneur, the man of business (or intellectual) agility now beholden to his own judgment, his own notions of what is desirable, possible, permissible. In the midst of such shifts not only in commerce but in sensibility, in the moral life of towns and cities, in a nation's social and cultural assumptions, all sorts of individuals struggle to consolidate their reputations, or fail quite evidently to do so. Eliot brings Dr. Lydgate in touch with Bulstrode, the doctor who is beholden to the banker, and further connects them through the potentially troublesome drunkard Raffles, whom Lydgate attends during what proves to be his final hours. Bulstrode, of course, hopes that Raffles won't pull through—that his physician won't work strenuously to pull him through. Meanwhile, awaiting the medical outcome, he goes through a spiritual crisis that evokes this characterization: "Strange, piteous conflict in the soul of this unhappy man, who had longed for years to be better than he was—who had taken his selfish passions into discipline and clad them in severe robes, so that he had walked with them as a devout squire, till now that a terror had risen among them, and they could chant no longer but throw out their common cover for safety."

Such anguish naturally brings the reader closer to this man whose darker side is not heinous, and not different in kind, surely, from that of many people of substance, but whose efforts at self-improvement (not in the contemporary, superficial sense of that phrase) attest to a moral scrupulosity of some considerable strength. It is noteworthy that Eliot does not investigate Dr. Lydgate's inner life with the kind of energy she devotes to Bulstrode's—when she might well have done so: the former is taking care of the unconscious Raffles, even as he very much needs a loan from Bulstrode, and in his capacity as Raffles's attending physician gets that loan, hitherto denied him. The moral burden is placed squarely on Bulstrode's shoulders, and his response to it is constant supplication of the Lord. He prays and prays; he confronts his not so secret wishes (that Raffles die) but also is aware of the utterly self-serving nature of such a desire. He is caught, that is, between a craven opportunism and a distraught realization of precisely that. He hopes that fate (maybe boosted by a doctor's inclination not to go the last mile for someone not especially important, indeed, down-and-out) will solve this threatening crisis of exposure. Yet he holds to the earnest conviction that he dare not intervene, try to hurt the sick and vulnerable Raffles, and not only for fear of potential harm to himself but, as Eliot suggests, out of a long-standing attempt on his part "to be better than he was."

It is of no small significance that George Eliot uses words such as "soul" and "spiritual" and "prayers" in connection with Bulstrode, but not Dorothea Brooke or Dr. Lydgate or Will Ladislaw or Casaubon, other important figures in this wide-ranging chronicle, meant to be, as Henry James put it, "philosophic" in nature as well as alert to the social manners of a segment of English life. In one sentence, meant to convey a practical man-of-the-world nevertheless struggling hard with the demands of his conscience as well as his "native imperviousness," his canny wish to get successfully through yet another worldly challenge, we are told of his mind's alarm and fearfulness (as he wonders about the medical fate of a man who can hurt him) in a way reminiscent of Milton's religiously awake verse—as opposed to the shrewd, essentially secular (psychological and sociological) kind of analysis that, as a matter of fact, made the novel so appealing to the "advanced" cadre of the London intelligentsia: "Whatever prayers he might lift up, whatever statements he might inwardly make of this man's spiritual condition, and the duty he himself was under to submit to the punishment divinely appointed for him rather than to wish for evil to another— through all this effort to condense words into a solid mental state, there pierced and spread with irresistible vividness the images of the events he desired."

Why, then, is Bulstrode's essentially personal (and psychological) conflict, not unlike the many others so knowingly (in our sense of things) rendered in this novel, presented with such explicit resort to matters of the soul as well as the mind? No question, for Eliot characters such as Dorothea Brooke and Dr. Lydgate and even Casaubon are different from Bulstrode: they belong in the company of thinking people, individuals who have ideas of their own, who are not beholden to a biblical literalism once so influential. Actually, these are men and women who have no real attachment to church life; yes, they are capable of *considering* religious or even theological issues, but their daily life is essentially secular in nature. They represent the professions, the academy, the politically or socially engaged: people of "thought," of "training," for whom the past's spiritual anguish is absent; it has yielded to the intellectual and moral anguish of a secular society. In contrast, Bulstrode is of a "lower order": he is a mere businessman, an uneducated man who has been on the make, perhaps in his common life one of Eliot's "Christian Carnivora," but maybe not—they seem "higher" in social status, less connected, really, to the daily hurdle of keeping afloat (and then some) that ordinary working people must keep confronting. While Bulstrode is hardly an Isaiah, or a passionate Christian pilgrim, his moral anguish takes on a spiritual quality, and his very vulnerability, his lack of self-assurance, his social marginality, his intense fearfulness and sense of jeopardy, hearken back, as no other scene in *Middlemarch* does, to a long religious history of sinners in turmoil (not to be confused with wrongdoers in felt danger of exposure, condemnation, punishment).

In a sense, then, Bulstrode's crisis of the soul, remarkable for its singularity, enables Eliot to bid an old tradition of earnest theological introspection farewell, to give us, by implication, a forecast of the future: countless Middlemarches in which church attendance has become a social convenience or a mere duty or even a business maneuver, and in which psychology and social circumstance mean much—mean everything. She was, of course, not a theorist; in fact, she parodies theorists, mocks her own inclination to be one in her treatment of both Casaubon and Dorothea Brooke. Yet she understood the mind in precisely the way Freud did: we are told, in authorial asides, of "repressed desire," of "identity," of "unreflecting egoism," of "invisible thoroughfares which are the first lurking-places of anguish, mania, and crime." In the novel she wants to portray influential secular determinisms at work, those within us and those that come at us from the outside. With respect to the latter, every shading of class is attended, and all possible occupations, institutions brought in to the narrative. So are words such as "alienation," which (like the "unconscious") we of the late twentieth century have assumed as our very own, whereas they make themselves quite at home in this chronicle not of an immediate, late-nineteenth-century yesteryear but the by now dim past that preceded by many decades the emergence of writers such as Freud or Max Weber, not to mention George Eliot.

In the same decade, the 1870s, that gave us *Middlemarch*, another demanding novel of no mean prophetic capability appeared, George Meredith's *The Egoist* (1879), a devastatingly satirical analysis of privileged self-centeredness, and an effort, surely, to describe what was happening in England amidst its obvious economic and national successes: a boundless assertion of manipulative vanity on the part of some who had come to think of themselves as the very center of the universe—in a sense, the ultimate challenge to, defiance of, the Judeo-Christian spiritual ethic, for which such an attitude is but one more aspect of our sinful pride. Meredith was much influenced by evolutionary theory. In poem after poem Meredith emphasized our capacity to spring free of our limitations, to emerge gradually from one state of being to another. Not that such a collective fate is foreordained. He had read Darwin, had drawn the proper lesson, the lesson, actually, that novelists such as George Eliot and he had always known: that chance and circumstance, in all their complexity and unpredictability, determine so very much, no matter our conviction of a decisive capacity to make a difference in this life. Still, we can weigh in, exert ourselves—indeed, that is our biological and psychological and moral mandate: "Our life is but a little holding, lent / To do a mighty labour: we are one / With heaven and the stars when it is spent / To serve God's aim: else die we with the sun."

For Meredith such lyrical moments ("Vittoria," 1866) were intended to stress our potential membership in a broader community: our fellow human beings, to whom we give what we have—and so doing, achieve a kind of immortality quite unlike that evoked in churches and monasteries and cathedrals. In *The Thrush in February* (1885) he makes that point yet again; and just before he died he called the following his favorite passage of all the verse he wrote:

> Full lasting is the song, though he,
> The singer, passes: lasting, too,
> For souls not lent is usury,
> The rapture of the forward view.

Such a destiny is not exactly what the church fathers of early Christianity had in mind for us, nor their descendants in the Catholic Church, nor those reformist pastors, theologians, kings and princes and dukes who in their various ways gave the world the Protestant churches. Meredith's God was an abstract one—a notion, really, of nature become Nature, and a faith, really, in an evolving human awareness, in intellectual and moral exertion as God. In *The Question of Whither* (whose philosophical title alerts the reader to the serious discussion ahead) he makes this observation:

> Enough if we have winked to sun,
> Have sped the plough a season;
> There is a soul for labour done,
> Endureth fixed as reason.
>
> Then let our trust be firm in Good,
> Though we be of the fasting,
> Our questions are a mortal brood,
> Our work is everlasting.

Here is the Lord become Good; and that transformation is constantly taking place, enabled by those who do honorable, decent work: their toil, of mind and body, a consecration of sorts, rendered to the overall story of humankind, which is our evolving Good, which is God. In such an evolution, knowledge becomes Knowledge, science is regarded as Science, and, inevitably, the sacred becomes the secular:

> Now when the ark of human fate,
> Long baffled by the wayward wind,
> Is drifting with its peopled freight,
> Safe haven on the heights to find;

Safe haven from the drawing slime
Of evil deeds and deluge wrath;
To plant again the foot of Time
Upon a purer, firmer path;

'Tis now the hour to probe the ground,
To watch the Heavens, to speak the word,
The fathoms of the deep to sound,
And send abroad the missioned bird.

On strengthened wings for evermore
Let science swiftly as she can,
Fly seaward on from shore to shore,
And bind the links of man to man.

There, in a piece of work titled "The Olive Branch" (a part of Meredith's first book, published in 1851), a young poet makes clear his conviction that somehow, through our own energies as they get usefully, thoughtfully deployed, we can soar, arrive Homeward, the Heaven of our planet become a Good Place. But a quarter of a century later, though he had not at all surrendered such a hope, Meredith was deeply troubled about possible (indeed, likely and all too evident) obstacles in such an imagined trajectory. He had taken a fuller, a more circumspect look at this human creature whose striving for knowledge he had chosen to praise, and concluded that there were other strivings at work in us, even in those who do, for sure, make this or that contribution to the world's growing body of discovered factuality. No doubt, too, he had looked around at the particular world he inhabited, one of relative comfort and accomplishment in (at the time) the richest and most powerful of nations—and seen plenty to give him concern: the craven and mean side of those who have no social or economic excuse for the way they elbow others, still, nor moral justification for the way they use their well-educated minds in the pursuit of their own purposes solely.

To take notice of such ambiguity in one's neighbors and friends and fellow citizens, and, not least, in oneself, is to risk the temptation of skepticism, first, then cynicism, then gloom. But Meredith (unlike Thomas Hardy, whose outlook in ways resembled his) was not prone to melancholy. He held steadfast, in his poetry, to a hopefulness about our prospects on this planet. He kept insisting upon our visionary side; and he never forgot how hard some people will work, how much of themselves they are willing to give, in factories and on farms as well as in libraries or laboratories. It was as if he, the versifier, owed us that realization: it was his responsibility to sing of our possibilities, our constant and heavy labor, often against substantial odds—to exult in us become exalted by virtue of our deeds.

But this poet also wrote novels and was known for his storytelling by many who had little or no acquaintance with his poems. In *The Egoist*, the most demanding and important of his fictional efforts, he didn't forsake altogether his optimism; he gave his readers a comedy—a contrast with Hardy's *Jude the Obscure*, wherein a poet's grave doubts about our future, about our capacity to manage our affairs sensibly and justly, became the energizing force in his expository writing. Meredith had no such grim intention when he constructed Sir Willoughby, who (in contrast to the humble, earnest, decent, idealistic Jude Fawley) is a rich nobleman, highly educated, quite charming, spirited and engaging, and by no means dumb either intellectually or socially (as are some others he encounters who belong to the same background he claims). Meredith is at pains not to let Willoughby have more authority than seems appropriate for a novelist who wants to mock a psychological inclination rather than explore it sympathetically. Still, the mere narration, at length, of a character's self-centeredness risks eliciting its own kind of tolerant understanding, if not pity, in the reader, even if Meredith has no affection at all for Willoughby, and the novel that tells of him has a title not meant to be laudatory, or even neutral in its significance. In a critical chapter (39), called "In the Heart of the Egoist," the philosophically mature poet tips his hand: "We are on board the labouring vessel of humanity in a storm, when cries and countercries ring out, disorderliness mixes the crew, and the fury of self-preservation divides: this one is for the ship, that one for his life." Of course Willoughby's notion of "self-preservation" is his very own: an egoist's requirement that anything and anyone in the proverbial way bend or bow out or be done with. Others are seen as desirable instruments of one's affirmation or as troubling presences precisely because they fail to defer, to placate, to oblige. "Consider him indulgently," the narrator asks of us, and then this: "The Egoist is the Son of Himself. He is likewise the Father."

This is unsettling language—it is not unlike that used in Christian theology—and Meredith has used capital letters for both Son and Father. He doesn't, though, pursue that angle of inquiry or comparison; if he had, he'd have no doubt wanted to shift the implied meaning of the word "Egoist," to strip it of its pejorative implications, so that he could then, as the theologian Karl Barth did half a century later, speculate on God's psychology—the utter aloneness of Him and His Son, and, so, the Egoism that inevitably develops in Them: an existential Egoism, or, maybe better, a transcendental Egoism. But Meredith was not trying to leap into Heaven knowingly, provocatively. Indeed, for him, Heaven is right here on earth, hence the high stakes of our behavior with one another. For God and His (only begotten) Son to be Egoists is a matter of theological phenomenology; for Willoughby or the rest of us to slip that far into ourselves is a thoroughgoing slide backwards, a moral reversion: "The Egoist is our fountainhead, primeval man: the primitive is born again, the elemental reconstituted. Born again into new conditions, the primitive may be highly polished of men, and forfeit nothing save the roughness of his original nature."

Meredith makes no attempt to spare Willoughby a good deal of highly critical regard and even flirts with the word "degenerate" as a descriptive term, lest we the readers miss the essential point of this book, a biography of an imagined sensualist trapped irrevocably in his own self-regard: ". . . he has entered the upper sphere, or circle of spiritual Egoism: he has become the civilized Egoist; primitive still, as sure as man has teeth; but developed in his manner of using them."

For the most part, in this novel, we are spared such sweeping broadsides. The juxtaposition of "spiritual" and "Egoism" may be confusing; the point is to stress

the rarefied or highfalutin nature of such self-preoccupation, a matter of class—though the creator of Willoughby, no doubt, might have observed the occasional
minister or teacher or doctor who would qualify as Willoughby's identical twin psychologically. We are being
reminded constantly in this novel that all the social and
cultural refinement in the world is quite compatible
with what in the Bible gets called "pride," with its
connotation of the sinful, the smug, the self-absorbed.
Meredith lacks the desire, though, to make his central
figure in any way tragic; rather, he seems to be indicat-
ing, the heart of the matter is precisely that: insofar as
one is an Egoist, one lacks the qualities that can make
for a person in some manner impressive or worthy of
serious attention, however flawed. This is a novel of
deadly superficiality, a story meant to make the serious-
minded reader (and, especially, the reader who knows of
Meredith's morally energetic poetry) shudder with apprehension, lest he or she be in the least jeopardy of
Willoughby's fate.

In 1978, at a meeting of the William Alanson White
Psychoanalytic Institute in New York City, I described
an experience I had had as a medical student at the Co-
lumbia-Presbyterian Medical Center in New York City.
I was asked to draw blood from an elderly woman
named Karen Horney who was dying of cancer. I knew
that she was a psychoanalyst, that she had authored several books which had been widely read—and that she
had little time left. I can still remember her quiet stoi-
cism as we made our rounds, trailing after the great (and
sometimes intimidating) Robert F. Loeb, the Bard

Professor of Medicine at Columbia's College of Physicians and Surgeons, and I can still remember Dr. Loeb's glancing at what she was reading, a book perched on her bedside table, George Meredith's *The Egoist*. He said nothing when he first noticed the book, and I said nothing a couple of days later when I met the same reserved but gracious lady at seven o'clock in the morning, my tourniquet in hand, and with it a tray containing syringes, test tubes, labels. Unlike some patients, Dr. Horney never flinched or murmured as I did my work; and when it was over, she thanked me, a rare event in such a line of work. She asked me a question or two about myself—where I came from, where I'd gone to college, what I'd had for a major—and when I told her I'd studied English literature, she asked me if I'd read Meredith's *The Egoist*, for which she then reached. Yes, I had; but I remembered, even then, only a few years afterwards, very little of what I'd read. She smiled, said she could understand why so little had stayed with me. I told her that, in contrast, I remembered some of Meredith's poems, and I attributed that recall to the virtues of a particular professor, Hyder Rollins, whose course on Victorian poetry I'd taken. Again she smiled graciously, nodded her head, but added a brief comment I've never forgotten: "I don't think Meredith would *want* you to remember this novel"—whereupon, I can also still remember myself thinking: for heaven's sake, then, why is she reading it, and of all times, now!

Dr. Horney seemed to know what was crossing my mind; at that time in my life I didn't realize how often individuals doing her kind of work invited the unspoken thoughts of those with whom they conversed. She spoke as if I'd actually said what I'd thought, as if she, too, had said as much to herself: "A patient of mine, a woman, kept mentioning this novel; she said it described her former husband 'to a tee.' I kept telling her I'd read the novel—I wanted to, but I never had the time. Now I do!"

I recall feeling sad then; I figured that she was nearer to death than she might want to believe, that she didn't actually have as much time as she assumed was hers. But she caught me up, yet again: she told me with no evident anxiety or fear or trembling that she might just make it through *The Egoist,* and maybe one other novel. She added that she was glad that she had the good sense to be reading fiction, not psychoanalytic journals or textbooks—and then these words, still strong in their impact, meaning, as I summon them, in their substance, from the distance of over four decades: "In this novel we are told about someone who is completely alone in the midst of all the company he keeps. That is what happens when you are an Egoist—you are deaf to anyone's avowal of love, and you have no voice of conscience addressing you. So, there is only silence."

Later that day I sat in my dormitory room in Bard Hall, looked at the Hudson River, kept hearing her in my mind say what she'd spoken earlier in that room, and wrote what I'd remembered in a letter to my brother Bill, who was then a graduate student in English literature, specializing in nineteenth-century poets, such as George Meredith. That way, and in subsequent conversations with him (he is a professor of

English now) I kept in my mind the brief encounter, so touching, even haunting, with someone whom I would later know as an important person in what became my own profession. No question, Meredith's Willoughby is beyond the heard call of others, hence his rock-bottom aloneness. Very important, he has no real conscience, as Dr. Horney was shrewd to emphasize: conscience as the voices of others who live inside us, their pleas and misgivings and worries and injunctions and admonitions all become ours to attend, to heed. In the absence of those voices, in the presence of a tenacious will geared to appetites cultivated amidst a rich life, the prepossessing Willoughby enacts his constantly insistent, exaggerated amour propre. He goes through the motions of engagement with others. He seems to struggle for the love of others, and he is a conventional person, to all appearances, not inimical to church and state, willing to defer to established customs, rules, laws. But he is the opposite of his creator's ideal—Meredith had high moral aspirations for himself and his readers: that each of us work hard on behalf of one another, that we be members of a community (village, borough, nation), an affiliation of mind and heart. These enlightened ones he celebrated: "They see how spirit comes to light, / Through conquest of the inner beast, / Which measure tames to movement same, / In harmony with what is fair. / Never is earth misread by brain: / That is the willing of her, there / The mirror: with one step beyond, / For likewise is it voice."

The title of that poem is "Hard Weather," and the poet has no doubt that it is difficult to put aside one's self, more than occasionally, in favor of a commitment to others. In *The Egoist*, he shows just how tempting that "suck of self" (a phrase coined by the novelist Walker Percy) can be, and not only for Willoughby. To make *The Egoist* a comedy is to stress the offhand, the unsurprising: the commonplace temptations rather than the singular disaster of a tragedy. A writer who is a moralist pulls his punches, lets the "inner beast" strut and swagger and seek its prey—in the hope that we readers will sweat gratefully as we take our measure of what distance separates us from Willoughby and his ilk. In a sense, I would only much later realize, Dr. Horney was getting her own distance from the "egoism" with which she constantly had to contend as a psychoanalyst. There, in the hospital, she could glimpse, at a remove, "the neurotic personality of our time," as she had described the psychological exiles and fugitives who by wrapping themselves in a host of "defenses" and "symptoms" had become substantially severed from participation in Meredith's "Earth," by which he meant Nature at its most productive: people joined in a harmony of embraced interdependence. Her patients came to her, so often, as Willoughbys, and she (like Meredith) had to take their measure but also do her best to help them out of their solipsistic ways, their belief not in God or even their fellow human beings but themselves only. Dr. Horney's phrase "our time" was meant to link the private conflicts of individuals ("the neurotic personality") with larger social and cultural developments—a linkage both Meredith and George Eliot fully appreciated, hence the "unreflecting egoism" of *Middlemarch* and the title and full text, as it were, of Meredith's novel: the Willoughbys whom a secular society (no longer beholden to the sacred) more than tolerates, encourages, as in the historian Christopher Lasch's phrase "the culture of narcissism."

Well before Dr. Horney and Professor Lasch worried publicly about the "egoism" Eliot wryly observed, Meredith sardonically evoked, the nineteenth-century poet and novelist Thomas Hardy registered a prophetic and tough and sometimes melancholy analysis of what he took the trouble to examine closely: the decline of religious conviction, spiritual faith, their replacement by a rationalism, a secular devotion to the factual, the provable, the self as our only sovereign—but at a considerable cost. In *Jude the Obscure*, his last novel (1895) he gives us a decent, aspiring country lad who gets smitten by the educational muse and takes himself to Christminster, a thinly disguised Oxford. There Jude is soon enough brought up short, disillusioned. Before he left on his pilgrimage (education as a way to God's grace), he had to "smother high thinking under immediate needs"—he and the vast majority of the world's people, still. But once he has come within the sight of this great university, where all that "high thinking" goes on, he is soon enough disappointed: "Only a wall divided him from those happy young contemporaries of his [the students] with whom he shared a common mental life: men who had nothing to do from morning to night, but to read, work, learn, and inwardly digest. Only a wall—but what a wall!"

To be sure, Hardy is remarking on class, on the way privilege separates those who have it from others, even in a university, ostensibly a place devoted to the intellect's work. But gradually the reader's sympathy for a yearning Jude (so very determined to make much of himself as a student) acquires a companion attitude, scorn for those who will have no part of the world's Judes: "He was a young workman in a white blouse, and with stone dust in the creases of his clothes and in passing him they did not even see him, or hear him, rather saw through him as through a plane of glass at their familiars beyond." Here the divide of class becomes something psychological rather than sociological: the narrator asks us to shift our attention from the unnoticed to the unobservant, from the invisible by virtue of social rank to the blind by virtue of a kind of sinfulness, which he persists in exploring. While we are told that Jude "was rather on an intellectual track than a theological [one]," we soon begin to realize that the two are not so readily distinguished, separated. Jude sees about him all sorts of reminders of Christianity—in stories, and, of course, in the form of churches, chapels. He is visiting with his own religious past and with that of his countrymen as he waits to hear whether he will be accepted for a course of study at this old university whose own past, also, is intimately connected to the history of the Christian Church in England.

Soon enough he has his much anticipated news, sent to "Mr. J. Fawley, Stone Cutter" (Hardy himself had been an artisan, a stonecutter, an architect's assistant, in his youth). He is told that he ought to remain in his "own sphere," stick to his "trade" rather than adopt "any other course." The narrator calls that "a hard slap"; soon Jude is at a bar tossing down some beer. Soon, as well, he is engaged in a broad and deep social and moral inquiry: "He began to see that the town life was a book of humanity infinitely more palpitating, varied, and compendious than the gown life. These struggling men and women before him were the reality of Christminster, though they knew little of Christ or Minster. That was one of the humors of things. The floating population of students and teachers, who did know both in a way were not Christminster in a local sense at all."

Hardy doesn't let the matter drop there, however. He has delivered, through Jude, a populist broadside, meant to expose the snobbery and insularity of a particular institution: its sanctioned arrogance and the smug egoism thereby generated in its teachers and students. He wants to go further, though, and does so by having Jude take action rather than merely mull things over with growing indignation: "The gates [of the university] were shut, and, by an impulse, he took from his pocket a lump of chalk, which, as a workman, he usually carried there, and wrote along the wall: 'I have understanding as well as you; I am not inferior to you. Yea, who knoweth not such things as these?!'—Job xii.3."

Early in the novel Jude is a "Christian young man"; he is "one who wished, next to being a scholar, to be a Christian divine." We are told that he "limited his reading [for awhile] to the Gospels and Epistles." No wonder, then, that the Bible haunts him in his hour of extreme disappointment; and no wonder that he calls upon Job, as he chalks his message on a university's walls. Jude's religious life, his deeply felt intimacy with the Bible, his hope to minister unto others in the name of Jesus Christ, his desire to learn not for learning's sake but the Lord's, comes to naught, and thereafter a life steadily deteriorates. *Jude the Obscure*, published as Freud was writing his greatest book, *The Interpretation of Dreams*, spells out a journey from religious piety, humbly pursued, to a psychopathology become a dominant aspect of daily life. Where once there was almost a naive trust in the Book of books, and all its stories, its lessons, its promises and warnings, its instances and remonstrances, now there is a growing, idiosyncratic defiance of the customary, justified by a realization of its rot, its large reservoirs of hypocrisy and pretense, its vainglory (to use a word commonly summoned back then). The second half of Hardy's novel offers betrayals, mental deterioration, infanticide, all that Freud tried to understand—his very effort to do so attentively watched, increasingly hailed, because, as Hardy noted (the point of his novel), a culture no longer powerfully, convincingly devoted to the "sacred" (with respect to its assumptions) was now becoming entranced by (what else?) the hereabouts (as against heaven and hell): the mind and its workings; society and its ills as *they* (not God's will or grace or mysterious reasons) shape our personal and collective destiny.

No question, Hardy the poet (as was the case with Meredith) struggled more privately, less stridently, to make his moral and philosophical points. For one thing, his poetry earned him less attention: he could have his vigorous say without the uproar that accompanied the appearance of *Jude the Obscure*. Indeed, the bitterness shown that novel by critics was not unlike the reception given Freud through much of his career—for daring to say what seemed so obvious and prevalent.

During his long writing life Hardy the poet constantly struggled with the biggest possible questions: what to believe, and why, and how to live, and with which day-to-day convictions? He was not afraid to use poetry as an instrument of cultural reflection. In "The Respectable Burgher on 'The Higher Criticism'" he confronts traditional biblical faith with a late-nineteenth-century scientific outlook:

> Since Reverend Doctors now declare
> That clerks and people must prepare
> to doubt if Adam ever were;
> To hold the flood a local scare. . . .

By the end of the poem the Bible's events, once invested with mystery and handed down as articles of faith, become mere stories—evidence, actually, of a superstitious past, and so this concluding self-description, if not avowal:

> Since thus they hint, nor turn a hair,
> All churchgoing will I foreswear,
> And sit on Sundays in my chair,
> And read that moderate Voltaire.

No question, Hardy, more than any of the Victorian poets (all of whom, in various ways, responded to the increasing confrontation of religious authority by rational, scientific thinking), explicitly sets aside the traditional view of God's ultimate authority in favor of an outright agnosticism. One of his poems is even titled

"God's Funeral," its message that of a reluctant but necessary farewell to religious faith as idolatry. The poet becomes a social historian, sketches the long haul of things, tells of a decisive shift in the relationship between secular knowledge and an adherence to sacred tenets:

> Till in Time's stay less stealthy swing,
> Uncompromising rude reality
> Mangled the Monarch [God] of our fashioning,
> Who quavered, sank; and now has ceased to be.

A hundred years later, we of this second half of the twentieth century would talk of a "God Is Dead" theology as if it were a new intellectual presence among us, but Hardy knew, under less favorable social and intellectual circumstances, where a scientific secularism was taking not only thinkers and writers, such as himself, but the millions of people for whom, he understood, that matter of "how to bear such a loss" was serious indeed.

In fact, he himself never quite reconciled himself to that "loss." True, he sounded the note of freethinking, contemporary candor; he gave us in verse the Bible as ancient fancy, no longer capable of holding us in real awe, no matter our persisting pretensions, protestations. In the daily clutch of things, we grab for the artifacts of Science and thereby acknowledge in our deeds what we may not want to (dare to) put into words. True, sophisticated minds, unable to accept a personal God or the immortality promised by many religions (certainly by the Christian faith), try to figure a way out of this impasse (as did Hardy himself toward the end of his life, and as do so many ordinary folk who recognize in their bones what, say, a Kierkegaard meant when he spoke of "the leap of faith," that big stretch required for the mind to make). In the midst of the darkness science both asserts and explores, we crave whatever light we can make for ourselves, even if we do so as the proverbial whistlers (or, as the expression goes, with hope against hope). Upon Meredith's death, Hardy at least allowed us (himself) this kind of afterlife:

> Further and further still
> Through the world's vaporous vitiate air
> His words wing on—as live words will.

If Hardy's rational, skeptical mind prompted a refusal of Christian faith in its customary institutional existence, and if his deeply felt social conscience, his energetic moral life, prompted his forceful confrontation, in prose and poetry, of the world's various duplicities, injustices (the phoniness he was so quick to render, mock), the part of him that, like Jude, kept hoping for a more honorable and decent world also exerted an influence on his thinking and writing, both. That being the case, he could turn utopian, or he could yearn for a God he didn't believe existed, the God of the Hebrew Prophets, the God of a Christ vividly awake to the world's various inequities, injustices. In a fascinating poem, titled "1967," he dared imagine our very recent time with some optimism:

> A century which, if not sublime,
> Will show, I doubt not, at its prime,
> A scope above the blinkered time.

Moreover, in the long haul of his life, he could not really abandon religion. His description of himself reading Voltaire can be interpreted as a provocative scientific or secular triumphalism; but one can as readily see the bleak and sad side to such a self-portrait and, too, the facetious side to a moment of lyrical sport. Here, in prose, in a work titled, no less, "Apology," he attempts a muted, tentative reconciliation: "It may be a forlorn hope, a mere dream, that of an alliance between religion, which must be retrieved unless the world is to perish, and complete rationality, by means of the interfusing effect of poetry." A determined secularist worries about our hunger for the sacred, carves out a role for the poet as one who can, as it were, lift rationalities into the heights of a hope become exalted as Hope (affirmed and celebrated through word, song, ritual in the name of "religion")—the best a guarded late-nineteenth-century seer could do for himself, for his readers: offer the secular a carefully contemplated, regulated dose of the sacred, or, put differently, remind the sacred of its distinctly limited place in the thoroughly practical, rational life that would prevail from 1900 onward.

III

Where We Stand

2000

WHEN Thomas Hardy died, in 1928, Adolf Hitler and his Nazi thugs were well on their way from political obscurity—one of a young republic's fringe groups—to major national authority. Less than five years later, the nation of Goethe and Schiller and Heine and Thomas Mann and Beethoven and Brahms, and, yes, the nation of Einstein, the nation in whose language Freud wrote, the nation of science and social science, of medicine and engineering and architecture (as in the Bauhaus movement) would be on its terrible way to the responsibility for tens of millions of deaths: on the battlefield, from relentless bombing, and, not least, in the concentration camps, whose enormous capacity for mass murder was enabled by the modern technology of a nation as "advanced" and "intellectual" as any in the world. Indeed, toward the end of the Second World War, many scientists who had fled Germany were now able to help the United States by drawing on their knowledge of theoretical physics and thereby, in a resort to applied physics, creating the nuclear bomb: science now the proven potential enabler of the entire world's destruction. Such an outcome, less than half a century after both Meredith and Hardy were here on earth, singing their faith in a growing accumulation of knowledge, would give pause to some of their heirs. The poet William Carlos Williams, for example, in *Paterson* (the first two books were published immediately after the Second World

War) worried long and hard about the historical ironies this century, then only halfway along, had visited on mankind: erudition, even in the humanities, even in poetry, could not (as with his friend Ezra Pound) offer any immunity to hate, to treason; scientific achievement could become in various ways and for various reasons an instrument of widespread death; aesthetic and intellectual refinement could prompt an indifference to social reality. No wonder, then, the vigorous, intense, unsparing, arguably overwrought assault on higher learning, on university life, in the third part of the first book of *Paterson*:

> We go on living, we permit ourselves
> to continue—but certainly
> not for the university, what they publish
> severally or as a group: clerks
> got out of hand forgetting for the most part
> to whom they are beholden.
> Spitted on fixed concepts like
> roasting hogs, sputtering, their drip sizzling
> in the fire.

How well I remember my visits, as a medical student, to Dr. Williams at his home, 9 Ridge Road, Rutherford, New Jersey—the urgent passion of his remarks as he tried to confront a young person's enthusiasm and expectations with the sober lessons acquired by a physician and poet in the course of a long life devoted to ordinary people in need of medical care and to a bravely original-minded writing of verse, of fiction, of nonfiction. As he drove (he was always pulling ahead of slow-moving cars), he told me of Joseph Goebbels, his Ph.D.

in comparative literature from Germany's august Hei-
delberg University; of Heidegger, the great philosopher
who had embraced Nazism unapologetically; of Jung,
whose psychoanalytic creativity didn't deter him from
a murky involvement with Nazi-controlled psychiatry;
and, again and again, of his longtime friend Ezra
Pound, whose descent into madness had been so viru-
lently mean-spirited in its character. But he didn't stop
there, with the celebrated, the gifted; he mentioned the
thousands of doctors and lawyers and college professors
and scientists, and, alas, the ministers and priests who
fell in with the Nazis, did their bidding, wore their
swastikas, shouted their "Heil Hitlers!" Once, seeing me
sag under all that new knowledge, and the explication
of it (I had heard a running commentary of the first
decades of this century), he stopped himself cold, became almost fiercely terse: "This secular mind—where
it's taken us."

I didn't know where to go with that remark. As with
others he uttered, I sat and listened in stunned silence,
and then I asked the naive questions that told of a lucky
innocence, no matter my college degree and my on-
going postgraduate education. This time, he pulled
himself back from a certain destination, expressed reservations about his own remark: "I'm in deep water
here—it's very complicated." I didn't know how to pursue the matter; I wasn't then privy to his line of thinking. Abruptly, we'd arrived in his beloved Paterson, and
his patients were now in his thoughts—as I learned
when he started telling me of one of them, a child we
were about to visit at his home. Later, I wrote down the
words I'd heard; and still later, while learning to be a

pediatrician, and anxious to have Dr. Williams's voice "on the record," to share it through a taped interview with my fellow hospital residents at a seminar entitled "Medicine and the Humanities" in which we were participating, I would return to that same subject, and hear this: "[Through] all these years of my practice I've heard parents talk about what they want for their kids. They want everything [for them], of course, but they're no fools: they know the score, they know what's ahead. Why wouldn't they—they're living 'close to the bone.' You know what? A parent's job—a mother's, a father's—it's to teach the kid to join the club, be an American. Now, what does that mean? This isn't the America of farming and trading and the church; or of the factory life and the church. People still go to church, but the God they worship (if they do [that] while they're sitting in those pews) isn't 'The Big Man' in their lives after they leave and go home. I've seen that happen; I've watched people who have just come here from Europe figure out how to be a Catholic, lots of them, and be an American. At first it's hard, they see the conflict, and they're torn. But it doesn't take long; I'll tell you that—in no time, you've got the kids growing up in *this* country (the way it's become), and that means they hear the bells, the church bells, sure they do, but they read the [news]papers, and they listen to the radio, and they pass the stores and look at the displays—and don't forget this: so do the priests. The bells are there, but there's a lot of other noise in the air, voices with messages about buying and selling: spend and get—and work hard, so you can spend more, get more, and hey, that's the life.

"This is a here-and-now world, that's what I mean when I say 'secular'; and the religious side of it, even the moral side of it—well, there's a lot up for grabs. You want an example of what I mean? [I had appeared perplexed, even overwhelmed by the sweeping nature of his remarks, and wasn't sure what to say, or ask, in response to them.] A grandmother, a young one, who was born in Italy and came here when she was fifteen, and married and brought up a family, and now is helping her daughter bring up another one, told me a few weeks ago that it's become different going to church here than it was when she was in Italy and when she first came here. She used to sit there and talk to God, and try to figure out what He wanted, and try to please Him. Now, she says, she mostly thinks about what's going on in her life, in her kids' lives, and she asks God to make it better. You know what? She got herself so damn close to being as smart as the big-shot social critics and philosophers—she said to me: 'It used to be I prayed to God, that I would learn what *He* wanted from me, and how *He* wanted me to behave (I wanted His help to be that kind of person, the kind He wanted); but now I pray to God that He help us with this problem, and the next one—to be a Big Pal of ours! It used to be, when I prayed to God, I was talking to Him; now, it's me talking to myself, and I'm only asking Him to help out with things.'"

A long silence, as he caught his breath and watched me as I tried to figure out, in mid-twentieth-century America, at the age of twenty-seven, where we were headed in this "interview." He must have noticed that I needed some summing up, a more conceptual or analytical posture on his part, as opposed to that of the story-teller, the narrator who "merely" describes what he has seen or heard, in the hope that his listener will get the point, use it in whatever way he or she likes (including as grist for the spinning of theory). Finally, I hear this: "You see, in a secular world, you think of yourself, your family, and friends; you pray *for* yourself, your family, and friends. I don't mean that you're not being truly religious that way—I guess I'm just trying to let you know what parents have been letting me know, that there's a shift going on, there's been a shift, and they can sense it, and they're as smart as you and me and some college professor in sociology or theology, who's trying to tell his class what's happening in our country. We've gone whole hog for 'the things of this world,' and that [attitude] is what a secular life is all about, and it's part of a person's religious life, too."

I now wanted to hurry us both back to his poetry, where I felt much more at home than I had been with the direction our conversation had taken. I made reference to his poem "The Catholic Bells," its ringing affirmation of a summoning institutional presence among modest, decent people going through the rhythms of their everyday lives. Yes, he appreciated my mention of that particular poem; it had given him much pleasure to write it, and he certainly was acknowledging the authority, both joyous and grave, of a powerful religion in the affairs of those he had known so long as a home-visiting physician (in the phrase then used, a "general practitioner"). But, I was reminded, he said at the start of the poem that he was an outside observer ("Tho' I'm no Catholic I listen hard when the bells / in the

yellow-brick tower / of their new church / ring down
the leaves / ring in the frost upon them / and the death
of the flowers . . . ”); and he was at immediate pains to
mention a “new church,” and to connect this church to
nature’s events, which, of course, would include our
human experiences:

> . . . the new baby of Mr. and Mrs.
> Krantz which cannot
> for the fat of its cheeks
> open well its eyes, ring out
> the parrot under its hood
> jealous of the child
> ring in Sunday morning
> and old age which adds as it
> takes away. . . .

Moreover, he reminds me, those Catholic bells are ringing, the poet insists, for

> the children of my friend
> who no longer hears
> them ring but with a smile
> and in a low voice speaks
> of the decisions of her
> daughter and the proposals
> and betrayals of her
> husband’s friends. . . .

Here the poem moves from a portrayal of appearances
(the “painting of a young priest / on the church wall
advertising / last week’s Novena . . . ,” or “the lame /
young man in black with / gaunt cheeks and wear-
ing a / Derby hat, who is hurrying / to 11 o’clock

Mass . . .") to a look beneath the surface, into the heart, if not the soul, of things to be found within the hearing distance of those bells that are both commanding yet no longer heard, meaning heeded in connection with what happens personally (we today would say psychologically) in the course of any given day. Again, Dr. Williams's "You see," spoken to me as if he couldn't take for granted that I actually could perceive what he was trying to get across in either the poem or our conversation: "You see, I'm trying to make a distinction—I was in the poem, too: that the bells are a thing of beauty, and they *register* beauty (for the observer, surely) but they don't get to the very life they were originally meant to [touch]; they're part of our *adorned* life, its loveliness, but the soul's intrigue, the battles of the mind, the lusts, the wrongs, the conflicts, the hurts and worries—that's out of their range. Maybe, you could say, out of their depth—there's no longer that deep probe of religion into the churchgoer's heart."

So it goes in this secular society, Dr. Williams was saying, as that society becomes worked into our "heart," our thoughts and assumptions and aspirations and concerns as they become our mind. Not that secularism hasn't always been a part of the thinking life of even those very much struggling for faith. Indeed, as the Psalms keep reminding us, the search for that faith is not incompatible with a search for wealth and power: David was a mighty king, he who proclaims so passionately his desire to be a faithful servant of the Lord. In psalm after psalm pride and envy and vanity rear their all too human faces—evidence aplenty of how hard it was, way back then (as now), to keep one's mind on the transcendent when the tug of the imminent was (is) so compelling. True, Psalm 8 is heralded as an avowal of God's greatness, man's insignificance. But in a way the psalmist/poet is reminding himself (and, maybe, God) that human beings have their own great authority, that they have been "crowned," that "glory and honor" are theirs. Moreover, the exaltation of the Lord carries with it an implicit skepticism worthy of our contemporary existentialists: "What is man, that thou art mindful of him? And the son of man, that thou visitest him?" Here is the scientific mind at work, trying to locate man in relation to "all sheep and oxen, yea, and the beasts of the field, the fowl of the air, and the fish of the sea, and whatsoever passeth through the paths of the seas." That same mind is indirectly asserting itself, of course, not only by God's grace, but through its own exertions of language—it is consciousness that is the psalm's subject, consciousness and its discontents, hence the inquiry addressed to the Lord, but surely an inquiry that David and others in ancient times asked of *themselves* (the secular turn of thought): who are we? who can survey this world as we do, and leave a record, through words, of our musings, our wonder, our not so thinly disguised hesitations, doubts?

A version of doubt is spoken in the brief and affecting Thirteenth Psalm, a favorite of Calvin's: "How long, O Lord? Wilt thou forget me forever? How long shall I take counsel in my soul, having sorrow in my heart daily?" Here is our twentieth-century "alienated" man, an outcry of felt abandonment, an introspection of the grief-stricken who is alone. The echo of that psalm, of course, can be heard generations later, in Jerusalem, when the Galilean teacher and healer, nailed to the cross, asks the Lord why He has forsaken a faithful believer, now so ignominiously doomed. Well before his earthly demise at the hands of an empire's local administrator, Jesus had made clear, in his moral instructions, the distinction between Caesar's "things" and those of God—a point not lost on Luther who, however, also tried to merge the two worlds by connecting the ministry to the local "caesars" (in what is now Germany) whose purposes his pronouncements amply suited. Certainly the popes whose lived splendor Luther and Calvin found so unworthy of Jesus had also figured out a way to live well (enjoy their earthly, secular time of it) and do well (commit themselves to the sacred as priests become cardinals become heads of the Roman Catholic Church).

Yet long before the excesses of Rome in, say, the thirteenth or fourteenth century—the provocations that preceded Protestantism—there was a secular hustler who prospered in Rome. A thousand years earlier, in fact, during the fourth century, when Christianity had triumphed over the "paganism" of the Roman Empire, the man we now know as Saint Augustine would begin the sixth chapter of the sixth book of his *Confessions* with these words: "I was all hot for honors, money, marriage"—a remark that, at the least, ought to give us today some historical context for the word "yuppie." Over fifteen hundred years ago Augustine's "city of man" stood strong, even as he would struggle so hard with himself to enter the "city of God." The lasting power, actually, of the *Confessions* is testimony to their psychological and moral candor. Long before Freud portrayed the mind in turmoil, in constant conflict, Augustine of Hippo looked within himself and found plenty of lust and greed and assertiveness and envy striving for expression, even as he gave us a chronicle of conscience at work, sometimes falteringly, often mightily. Hence his emergence not as a big shot, an imperial functionary with lots of people shaking in their boots at his every word, but as a priest ready (no matter the conflict, the regrets) to surrender an active sexual life with a common-law wife (they had a son) and, too, all the blandishments of a secular life available in those last years of Rome's authority. He would live to learn that the Vandals had taken Rome (410) and, indeed, were closing in on his own city of Hippo when he died (430). His, then, was a story right out of our time—the *Confessions* give us "drives" and a vigorous conscience and, not least, the ego at work, taking measure of things both within its habitat, a particular mind, and without: a still great capital city, a still inviting world of commerce and military power, not to mention a religion (Christianity) itself commanding more and more influence. That ego's willfulness, its inclination toward the sacred, would eventually settle things, prompt a decided shift in the direction of a man's energies and, not least, an account of its own workings: the ninety-three books that a bishop of Hippo was "inspecting" (cataloging, we would say) at the very end of his life.

There are, of course, empires and empires—some of them a matter of land and treasure and people and military strength, some of them a matter of beliefs held, ideas propagated and accepted, values espoused with success. Augustine laboriously wrote his manuscripts by hand, and they were just as laboriously copied by others. They did not become "books," as we know them, in his lifetime or for centuries thereafter. In this regard (the matter of culture, and of technology as it affects not only the way we live but the thoughts we have) I leap from the seventh century, from the Christian bishop contemplating at the end of his life the work he did as a writer, to the second half of this twentieth century to which we have belonged—to a conversation with Anna Freud toward the end of her life (1973), when she was willing to recall her father's way of looking at his books in the last years of his life: "More than once my father remarked that if it hadn't been for the fact that his ideas became books, and those books were read all over the world—there would not have been what we now call 'psychoanalysis.' No, he wasn't referring to the spread of his ideas, not just that. [I had interpreted her words that way.] He wrote his ideas as they came to him; he was a doctor, who was learning as he did his work with patients, and then thought about what was happening between him and them. Once his manuscripts became books, the ideas in them were out in the world—they spread, and then he got letters from others, who were interested in what he said. Soon, they were visiting him, the doctors and the teachers and the artists and the writers. Those people had a strong influence on him, on what he thought and how he wrote.

"It is usually put the other way: Sigmund Freud and his 'circle.' But as we keep saying in our clinical work, let us turn the coin over [look at the subject under discussion from another vantage point]: until others came to work with my father, he was all alone, with no sense that what he had seen and come to believe had any value to others. He needed people who could share his ideas, make suggestions, give him a sense (how is it put these days?) of 'community.' I mean by that not only 'psychological support'; I mean intellectual solidarity: colleagues who give you a feeling of 'reality,' that what you have heard, and in your own mind concluded to be true, is in turn being heard by others, who have decided that it does, after all, make some sense! Otherwise, there is a danger that the one who is coming up with the ideas will begin to feel that he is not only alone, but alone with his 'fantasies.' I suppose that may be somewhat more tolerable for novelists—though they, too, want an 'audience.' But my father was a doctor, and he had done 'research' before he began to write his book on dreams, and he very much needed to know—how shall I say it?—that he wasn't dreaming about dreams! I remember how he felt when those who read his first book began to come to him through their letters, or in visits: it all became *real*—that is, not only something in his own mind, but something that belonged to the world."

Miss Freud was saying that in our time, more than ever, the ideas of individual writers can quickly become an important aspect of the thought of millions. Thus when George Eliot gives us Dorothea's "theoretic" mind, and George Meredith gives us Sir Willoughby's limitless "egoism," and Sigmund Freud gives us an explanation of how those aspects of our human psychology, and many others, work in our daily lives, the result is a widespread public knowledge—which has its own, enormous cultural significance. The secular world is hungry for breakthroughs such as Freud achieved, lives off them, regards them as a (temporary) guiding light. Here is Miss Freud, once more, looking back as a social historian, a cultural critic, at the relationship between the emergence of her father's ideas and the use to which they were put, not in clinical settings but as instruments of instruction in how to live a life (as a body of philosophical wisdom, really): "I recall, even in the early days [of her father's work and writing], the opposition; but I also remember how surprised he was at the way—how shall I say it?—his ideas took hold, caught on fire. It's a good thing there weren't phones then: they'd have been ringing all day and night! My father was pleased, but he was thoughtful enough—he had enough distance from his own ideas—to realize that, as he used to put it, 'something larger was going on.' He meant by that—he meant people were looking to psychoanalysis for something they weren't getting elsewhere. They weren't only interested in understanding the mind; they wanted answers to all the riddles of existence.

"At first, you know, he thought that [such an interest] was a sophisticated kind of 'resistance'—an attempt to distract us, divert us, from 'depth analysis,' from psychoanalytic investigation proper, you could say, into the 'murky reaches of philosophical speculation'—that was a phrase I recall Karl Abraham [one of Freud's colleagues] using once in a conversation. But gradually we all began to see that there was something missing in the lives of people, and that the 'problem' wasn't necessarily psychological—do you see what I mean? [I nodded a bit too quickly, thereby alerting Miss Freud's never dull or apathetic psychoanalytic antennae, and prompting her to stop for a second, look directly, carefully at me—as if to suggest that, of course, there *are* some people, in and out of the psychoanalytic fold, whose way of thinking might well fit Karl Abraham's description!] My father indicated his understanding [of this social and historical development] when he used the word *weltanschauung* in connection with psychoanalysis. He wasn't being presumptuous, as some of his critics asserted. He was acknowledging that for a lot of people psychoanalysis becomes not only a 'treatment,' as the doctors would say, but something much bigger and more lasting—it's *there* for the person long after he or she has stopped being an analysand, and become someone who has been analyzed. As a matter of fact, when he [her father] wrote 'Analysis, Terminable and Interminable,' the same kind of considerations had occurred to him: for some people analysis seems to go on and on, and if it may be that something has gone 'wrong' to explain that [outcome], it also may be that what has happened has been working out quite well for the person [analysand] in question and for the analyst, too. In earlier times they would be called 'wise friends' of one another!"

In her own way, Miss Freud was echoing, on that occasion, remarks she had made in her book *Normality and Pathology in Childhood*. There she had indicated at substantial length the nature of the "search" certain parents embarked upon, throughout the childhood of their sons and daughters, for this or that "technique" to ensure optimal psychological well-being. The point was somehow to find, as she once put it, "a perfect childhood"—and then, of course, her ironic comment: "As if there ever could be such a thing—and if there were, what would be wrong then, with the children and us!"

Still, she was not inclined to overlook the possible reasons for such a "search," such a desire on the part of the well-educated and well-to-do adults of the Western, industrial nations who were the clients, if not the clientele, of psychoanalysts. In a secular society many seek "guidance" (moral as well as clinical) from doctors, from psychiatrists and psychoanalysts, rather than the clergy, hence the eagerness of so many ministers, priests, rabbis to embrace "pastoral counseling." Of course, in the early days of psychoanalysis things were different. In that regard, Miss Freud could be quite unsparingly tough on her own colleagues. For instance, she reminded them (in an address before the New York Psychoanalytic Institute) that they were doing quite well financially, and were held in very high esteem socially, culturally, a contrast with the fate of the first analysts, who had to brave a kind of professional ostracism, both intellectual and even personal in nature: the shunning of a society still monarchical and religious in its upheld tenets.

Like others who shared a profession with her, she was struggling with the way a certain kind of work can be taken up, embraced not only as something useful or helpful but as a revered bedrock of one's believing life— hence the words of her onetime analysand, Erik H. Erikson, at the end of his first book, *Childhood and Society*, when he was trying to look at the qualities that characterized (by midcentury) those who chose psychoanalysis as a profession: "the various identities which at first lent themselves to a fusion with the new identity of the analyst—identities based on talmudic argument, on messianic zeal, on punitive orthodoxy, on

faddist sensationalism, on professional and social ambition—all these identities and their cultural origins must
now become part of the analyst's analysis, so that he
may be able to discard archaic rituals of control and
learn to identify with the lasting value of his job of
enlightenment."

Such a statement indicates, through the use of historically charged words (talmudic, messianic, orthodoxy) a
writer's conviction that impulses and goals and attitudes
once connected to Judaism, to Christianity, to institutionalized religious life, have now become connected to
a profession that is prominent indeed among the secular bourgeoisie. Another psychoanalyst, Allen Wheelis,
more than echoed Erikson's observations, also during
the 1950s and 1960s, in an article published in the *In-
ternational Journal of Psychoanalysis*, "On the Vocational
Hazards of Psychoanalysis," and in his first two books,
The Quest for Identity (a series of essays) and *The Seeker*
(a novel). Wheelis was interested in the way analysts are
(only for a while, one hopes) regarded as godlike by
their patients (transference) and by others as well. These
members of the second generation, as it were, of psychoanalysis were anxious to explore not only their profession but that world to which it had come to mean so
much. Here is how Erik H. Erikson put that matter: "I
came to America [in 1933] because Joan [his wife] was
Canadian, and had gone to school in New York [at Bar-
nard], and wanted to return—because we both saw
what even then was happening, the rise of Fascism. We
were also worried about the fate of psychoanalysis itself—it seemed to 'belong' to a relatively small group of
people [analysts] and, of course, their patients. But in

America, we soon saw something else—psychoanalysis had 'spread out,' all right, broadened. 'We' were everywhere: in the movies and in the universities, and in the theater, and in public forums and discussions, much more so on this side of the Atlantic than was ever the case in Europe. I would remember wistfully my words about Vienna—where I thought 'we' were becoming 'ingrown.' Now, 'we' were 'all over the place'—including the churches and synagogues!"

Such a development had to do, ironically, with faith, though the object of faith, in "the churches and synagogues" Erikson had mentioned, wasn't God and His judgments, Christ and His teachings, or a received spiritual tradition as it has become a sacred and cherished set of beliefs, rituals: a dogma held high, called upon daily in the course of a life. Rather, the faith was (is) that of a secular mind as it has developed over the centuries, and especially in this past one: the faith we have in science; the rise of the social sciences, and their sense of entitlement with respect to the credibility extended them, the expectations entertained of them—all of that being evidence of the faith we have in ourselves, in our ability to know ourselves, gain control of things (within and outside ourselves) through such knowledge. And increasingly these recent years, these last ones of a century, a millennium, it is a faith in the capacity of the human brain (the organ that has investigated successfully all other organs) to explore itself, understand itself fully, gain operating (clinical) control over its vulnerabilities, aberrancies.

There are, clearly, important consequences to such a shift in human knowledge and, correspondingly,

human allegiance. The Ego of the famous psychoanalytic triad has an increasing authority. In his more
hopeful moments (some would say naive ones, some
would say impossibly proud ones) Freud dared say,
"Where the Id was, there shall the Ego be"—an earnest
doctor's clinical dream, but maybe an exaggerated one
that reflected (in the spirit of those two well-known
concepts, transference and countertransference) the
shared desire of patients and their doctors: the desire to
have more control over desire. Eventually, Freud dared
prophesy, the Id, once possessed of such hidden power,
will yield increasingly to our biological scrutiny: psychoanalytic investigation a prelude to the biochemical
and neurophysiological kind.

With all of the above happening, the third agency of
the psychoanalytic paradigm, the Superego, has endured a shift in its overall strength, and in its relationship to the other two members of this psychological ruling junta: a diminished hold over the mind, an erosion
in its capacity to shape the Ego's activity, bear down on
that of the Id. It is the Superego, naturally, that has always linked us with persuasive strength, if not a decided
vehemence, to the world beyond the home, the world
of churches and synagogues and mosques, and, too,
of "culture" in all its manifestations: the printed word,
and painted canvas, and, these days, the photographs,
the movies and videos and television programs of our
heavily visual culture. Perhaps among individual psychoanalysts and their analysands, Freud's dictum held
even in the early years of this century—an Ego increasingly enhanced, fortified, braced by "insight" may well
have significantly laid low the Id. But among people

influenced culturally rather than clinically by psychoanalysis, the most immediate consequence was that of
an altered Superego, as Anna Freud once said (as did
Erik H. Erikson, many times).

For Miss Freud, at the end of her life, such a course
of events was both ironic and unwelcome: "Our first
patients [who came to see Freud and his followers in
Vienna and, later, Berlin, Budapest] were men and
women who were the victims of self-accusation, among
other things. They were men and women in whom the
Superego was highly developed, to say the least—over-
developed. They suffered from the judgments they had
learned to hand down on themselves—for 'crimes' they
had come to believe they had committed: the Superego
at work! (I am simplifying, but not all that much!) Over
the decades, I have seen the clinical picture change—
our patients are less and less overwhelmed by the power
of the Superego in their mental life. They have been
brought up differently [a contrast with what was once
the manner of rearing children]: they have been re-
assured and complimented, and given so many things,
so they know the meaning of yes, but not so much the
meaning of no, and, of course, some of them have
rarely, if ever, been told no—that they must *not* do this
or that. Nor have they been threatened or scolded
much—things were explained to them, over and over,
with great professed patience, and with much assurance
of the parents' love.

"I think I covered a lot of this in *Normality and Pathology in Childhood*—how, with the best of intentions,
many of the most progressive and enlightened parents
went out of their way to do everything in accordance

with the latest psychoanalytic principles, taking care of all 'needs' and anticipating all the anxieties and fears and worries that any of us could imagine or had seen in our work—only to have, as a result, not an absence of childhood difficulties (and worse) but a whole new order of them. Gone were the children deeply afraid of doing the wrong thing, or worried that they might slip up, get into serious trouble, or bothered by frightening thoughts or nightmares, in which they step over the bounds, and get punished severely [for doing so]. Now we have, even in our younger children, what has become mentioned by more and more of us in our clinical case conferences, the 'narcissistic personality.' These children aren't afraid of being caught, judged, sentenced, and punished by their conscience, their Superego; if they are afraid of anything (and some of them seem brazenly fearless!), they are scared that they will be able to do anything, that there are no limits.

"What then will happen? I recall describing that [state of affairs] in several papers and in the book [we'd been discussing *Normality and Pathology in Childhood*]: 'When . . . the severity of the Superego is reduced, children get the deepest, most troubling anxieties of all, the fear that they can't prevail against the pressures of their own drives,' words to that effect. [They were almost the exact words she used in the book.] That is, I think, what some of our contemporary philosophers are getting at, when they talk about their existential despair? I don't mean to speak for them; I have to admit, I haven't read them much but I do read *of* them, in the papers, and I hear of them, from friends and my analytic patients— and I think they are telling us that the old Superego is no longer around for them, and for a lot of others, and they are more and more 'rational,' thanks to psychoanalysis, I would suppose, and physics and biology, all we know today, and so 'everything goes,' as the expression says, all depending on your own choice. Even if you really don't *want* it so that 'everything goes,' and even if you know the dangers—you're hard put to build a series of prohibitions. On what will you base them? (What that you can defend, that is, in a logical argument?) We've come full circle, I'm afraid [the irony of her use of that last word!]: we started out trying to use our wits to help people be less anxious, less driven by a tyrannical Superego, and we've come to the point that people are more anxious and even alarmed and fearful, but not of the Superego, but of—themselves, their 'drives,' we say, or their 'situation,' their 'existential fate,' their 'nature,' others put it. How do people say it: live long enough!"

If God is declared "dead," if the Bible is regarded as a historical text, or a series of stories, all to be deconstructed, if religion is an "illusion," and if children are seen as our big hope, our only chance of a future life (lived through them), and as ones to be encouraged, enabled, given all possible intellectual and emotional leeway—small wonder that the Superego of old is gone, with its nays and oughts, its muscled insistence on prohibitions, requirements, amplified by commandments and encyclicals and powerful preaching and hymns sung or cantors singing, by the Talmud or the words of God become man, and now part of God again, by the believed presence of a hovering Holy Ghost that, as one child said to me years ago, "can see right through you, so there's no trick you can pull that isn't noticed" (he of working-class Catholic background). All of that religious tradition is a thing of the past for more and more people, even as that boy just mentioned would go to a first-rate high school, then to an Ivy League college, and lose interest in, retain only a nominal belief in, "the Holy Ghost."

Instead, we have, as Miss Freud adduced, a still energetic Id, our lusts and resentments and angers ever upon us, and a newly authoritative Ego, blessed with insights, a growing body of knowledge, a confident sense of more of both to come—and, yes, blessed with a faith of sorts, a faith in those insights, that knowledge is all-important. I believe this, each of us says: that over time an increasingly knowing human mind will prevail over nature's various mysteries, will see us exploring the heavens, conquering one disease after another, and, not least, gaining an understanding of its own workings, the mind, at last, its own master. Under such circumstances, our scientific investigators become more than mere allies of the Ego; they bring to it a potentially ruling authority. Once the Ego was a nervous and shaky negotiator, always worried about the censorious Superego, and always assailed by the demanding Id. How to placate conscience and allow for expression of desire—a lifetime's task! Now those self-directed and self-imposed judgments of the Superego are gentler, indeed, among many of the secular bourgeoisie, not to mention among many of the rich and poor as well. Now, too, we understand our emotional life as never before and, more and more each year, our brain's biological life: a new sovereignty for the Ego. The mind's psychological and biological investigators have become godlike for so many of us: the "transference" that elevated psychoanalysts to seers in the eyes of their patients and at the same time (a kind of "cultural transference") gave those individuals a broad recognition as pundits, prophets, secular priests of sorts. The case is similar today with the neurobiologists who are exploring the brain's biochemistry, neurochemistry, enabling a biological psychiatry of increasing credibility, competence.

Not that we have been unwilling in the past to grant certain individuals oracular power: theologians for some, saints for others, philosophers for still others, soothsayers and magicians of one kind or another. More recently, as Miss Freud and Erik H. Erikson remind us, we have watched the secular theories of Freud become invested with something more than enthusiastic interest, acceptance: a dogmatism, rather, that bespeaks adherence to a faith. Similarly with Marx's ideas—Lenin the political theorist and revolutionary figure become Lenin enshrined in a mausoleum, his every word worshiped. Nor are we incapable of going down the same road with respect to our neuro-psychopharmacologists. Already the pill Prozac has been on the cover of our newsmagazines, and one wonders whether some person, at some point in time that is not far off, will address us as a brain scientist but, soon enough, become as revered as Freud was, accorded a degree of respect that proves as confounding and embarrassing (and seductively inviting) as Miss Freud remembered such a development to have been for her aging father: "Toward the end of his life I was his secretary; I had to deal with his correspondence; and [so doing] I felt I was learning so very

much—I would say to myself that I was getting the biggest education possible. My father had become for a lot
of people someone who had discovered nothing less
than how the mind works, and since everyone is struggling in some way with how his or her mind works, the
Dr. Freud of Vienna, and then London, was the one
who had the answers—or the one who was the enemy,
if you believed that only certain other people have the
answers, whether they be scientists or philosophers or
religious figures. So, we received lots of attention; and
whether it was adulation or bitter scorn, each of those
reactions, by their intensity, told us what had happened
to an Austrian physician who tried to learn about how
we manage our psychological affairs!"

In a polite, wry manner Anna Freud was describing
herself as a witness to secular idolatry, even as she was,
also, in a position to observe the envies and rivalries that
can be stirred, as the expression goes, when a new kid, a
whiz of some kind, arrives on the block: who are *you* to
be telling others so much and, as a result, to have become the recipient of so much expressed allegiance! In
a sense Freud the self-described psychological "conquistador" became, inadvertently, an investigator whose
scholarship, in its reception among others, has taught us
more than he ever thought was possible: the relationship of psychoanalysis to our culture as itself a means of
understanding how the mind works—what we crave,
how we try to manage our yearnings and apprehensions.

With God gone for so many intellectual pioneers
of the last two centuries, the rest of us, as students
and readers, as seekers mightily under their influence,
have only ourselves left as "objects" of attention. The

theologians were supplanted by the philosophers, the religiously committed philosophers by the skeptical, secular philosophers, who, in turn, have been supplanted in worldwide influence by a biologist, an economist, a psychiatrist, a physicist, each of whom (Darwin, Marx, Freud, Einstein) has an inclination to be contemplative in a particular secular way: to wonder about things, about the secrets that await our triumphs of discovery. Human beings have thus come to be seen as Promethean deities of a distinctively hardworking and limited kind, inasmuch as they possess no magic, have only their wits as instruments of newfound comprehension, and are personally all too finite in the existence they have, by mere chance, luck, found for themselves.

In the long run of Western high thought, Pascal was the great transitional figure, the one who tried so arduously and ardently to uphold the sacred, to link himself with the Judeo-Christian apologetic tradition (and especially, with Saint Augustine's mix of the cerebral and the emotional), while at the same time acknowledging quite pointedly and bravely (especially for his time, maybe for any time) the secular claims of "reason." He evidently felt these claims pressing hard on his brilliantly knowing, reflective mind, hence his willingness in the *Pensées* to declare openly his rock-bottom materialism, even as (like a figure in a Chagall painting) he hungers for transcendence, tries to defy reason's gravitational pull, leap high toward a faith that will turn those "vacant, interstellar spaces" into a believer's green pastureland. Ultimately, though, his posture is that of resignation—a secular intellectual's version, really, of Kierkegaard's resignation: like Abraham, Pascal walks toward a God he *will* believe in, no matter his every doubt, his ample measure of disbelief. Thus the well-known pensée (278) that puts the split of secular/sacred right before us (before himself) with no effort at qualification: "It is the heart which experiences God, and not reason. This, then, is faith: God felt by the heart, not by reason." The Freud who explored human subjectivity so sensitively and sensibly, both, would perhaps have been more responsive to such a way of putting the matter, less driven by that approach to the combative truculence of *The Future of an Illusion*, which, in turn, became a hymn of sorts to his own faith: a Reason hugged with no worry of idolatry, with no regard for the crimes done in its name. (He, who admired Ibsen so much, might have taken to heart the riveting message of *The Wild Duck*: that inquisitive, explorative, insistent Reason can be callous, harmful in the extreme, because illusion systematically and ruthlessly stripped from someone can bring him down completely, prompting self-destruction—yet another of the Norwegian playwright's fiercely idiosyncratic reminders posed to a secular, modern world that flocked approvingly to his plays without, always, understanding the complexity and ambiguity of their message.)

In any event, at his most determinedly secular, Pascal knew to pull no (sacred) punches: "The last act is tragic, however happy all the rest of the play is: at the last act a little earth is thrown upon our head, and that is the end, forever." Those words are a precise avowal of the heart of secularism by a spiritually passionate scientist whose writings are part of a "sacred" literary and introspective tradition but are also candid in a way congenial to Freud and Ibsen, to the scientists who are the mathematician and biologist Pascal's contemporary heirs. No wonder, in that regard, the (also French) philosopher Simone Weil (like Pascal, she was plagued by an unquenchable rationalism that wouldn't, finally, yield to the invitations of the spiritual, however desperately sought) would call upon the haunting phrase in the 282d pensée, "waiting for God," with such intense longing. In a moment of unflinching candor Pascal brushed aside so very much (not least the ceremony and ritual and educational zeal of the Catholic Church) when he dared allow this with respect to rational man: "Therefore, those to whom God has imparted religion by intuition are very fortunate, and justly convinced. But to those who do not have it, we can give it only by reasoning, waiting for God to give them spiritual insight, without which faith is only human, and useless for salvation."

Those sentences convey a degree of psychological and philosophical complexity that, in its implication, is unnervingly agnostic, a prelude, way back, to "the modern age," whereof Kierkegaard spoke, though not that of the Copenhagen bourgeoisie, whom he so roundly detested. He was a virtual stand-in for Pascal. Really, both of them are psychologists, worthy predecessors of Freud, or for that matter Dostoievsky, who famously admitted that he'd keep believing in God, no matter what—no matter the capacity of anyone to prove such a conviction "false." Faith, then, becomes something beyond any semblance of rationality, "useless" in and of itself insofar as one's ultimate future is concerned.

Therefore Abraham's blind obedience to a hope, a hope of God's grace, really, in defiance not only of rationality but of all moral sense, as rendered in *Fear and Trembling*, and therefore, as well, Pascal's "waiting," precisely the descriptive word for what Isaac and his father endured upon that hill in the ancient Middle East.

All of the immediately above brings me to Walker Percy's home in Covington, Louisiana, in 1973, where we talked and talked about what he kept calling "American secularism," a version, obviously, of a larger phenomenon. But it was a version he was then regarding closely, in preparation for *Love in the Ruins*, where he took us all on, we who live now, in these last years of a century, and of the second millennium in the Christian scheme of things. In that regard, I remember his thinking of Pascal with special tenderness (and anxiety), and, of course, of Kierkegaard, whom he had read and read in the 1940s and 1950s, before his emergence as a novelist who kept trying to "illustrate" that Danish writer through the magic of storytelling. At one point Dr. Percy, a physician and metaphysician as well as a novelist, claimed this with great conviction: "The abstract mind feeds on itself, takes things apart, leaves in its wake all of us, trying to live a life, get from the here of now, today, to the there of tomorrow." He stopped— worried, I thought, that he might have gone too far.

But, in fact, he wanted to push his argument further, though with some needed qualifications: "Once we go down the path of abstraction we're taking moral risks, psychological risks. We become drunk on ourselves— full of ourselves. Sure, I'm being abstract a bit right now—I know: the sinner denouncing sin! I'm not

talking about something I don't know! I guess I'm trying to weigh the risks of doing what you've got to do.
We're the ones who do this—figure out the world. But
there ain't no free lunch: things cost, even one of the
best things we've got going for us, our ability to calcu-
late and move from the specific to the general. People
get carried away in lots of different ways, and we're usually good at spotting how the other fella is going wild,
but it's harder to get that kind of distance on yourself
and your kind of folks. I keep remembering Kierkegaard's gripe with Hegel—that he'd [Hegel] figured out
everything, with all the theorizing he did about history
and time and ideas and their impact on one another;
but he left out one thing, how it goes for people from
one day to another: the 'history' of someone getting
through an ordinary day. Kierkegaard loved irony—he
took it further: he was sardonic. He saw pretense all
over the place—and he saw it in his own head: the pretense of the theorist taking on so much that he loses
commonsense contact with ordinary human goings-on.
We build big skyscrapers of thought, huge telescopes of
visionary thought, but in our lives, we live in small bun-
galows or shacks.

"I know I'm being cranky about all this. I write all
these metaphysical pieces, and later I'll scratch my head
and try to figure out whether there isn't some other way
of getting the same point across—that's when I try to
tell a story. Yes, I know [I had diverted his train of
thought with an abstract remark about the difference
between analytic thinking and the narrative, expository
impulse], it's just two different roads you take. But
there are dangers in anything you do, and I think we

know from our critics the dangers in fiction, about how sloppy and unimaginative and confusing and 'unformed' a short story can be, or a novel—[we have learned all that] from those critics, who are using 'the analytic mode' [alas, my words] to comment on the guy who's telling himself a story, and handing it over to the reader for its pleasure, and sure, for the message it may have wrapped somewhere inside. But who takes on the critics—I don't mean a critic who writes a review of a novel, no. [I had asked whether that was what he meant.] I mean, the limits (in general) of critical thinking, abstract thinking—well, I'm struggling here: I don't mean 'limits,' I mean pitfalls. Yes, you can say 'hazards' [I'd volunteered that word].

"Let me try this on you: we ought to stop, every once in a while, and ask ourselves who we think we are. I'm not just talking 'existentialism,' here; I think I'm talking about moral self-examination—as in exactly who do you think you *are*?! There are times when we get so full of ourselves—we've 'lost all modesty.' I recall a teacher of mine in elementary school; she'd catch us being very 'clever,' lording something we'd discovered over everyone we could lay our hands on, and she'd call us to her, and she'd say: 'Now there, Walker, you sure are smart, you're clever as can be; and you're making sure everyone in the world knows it—the trouble is, *that's* not so clever, and it's not so nice, either, because you've lost all modesty.' I think I've got it down word-for-word."

There was more, much more; a man himself quite capable of extended conceptual riffs, some of which, frankly, I had found hard to fathom ("Towards a Triadic Theory of Meaning," or "The Symbolic Structure of Interpersonal Process," or "Semiotic and a Theory of Knowledge"), was seemingly turning on himself with a certain kind of vehemence, albeit rendered with a laid-back geniality. In fact, though, Dr. Percy was worrying about all of us, how we can use our minds in such a way that we lose respect for our friends, neighbors, and family members, even: a moral or spiritual kind of awareness forsaken for a bare-bones intellectual kind that is wielded rather than simply summoned.

In time I would let Dr. Percy's words settle in my head—a shrewd arrow directed by him at the apple of knowledge become something else: the sin of pride. He was "worried sick," he had said at one point, by the inclination of many of us, himself certainly included, to take ourselves away from the concrete particulars of a lived life (the hopes and worries and fears such a life prompts) in favor of an all-too-clever kind of conceptual analysis that gives short shrift to human experience (in all its complexity) as it befalls every person who is born, lives, and knows full well of death's certainty. In his own words, a summing up of what he'd been saying, he offered this "try," a most serious look on his face: "I don't mean to demean Intellect; that's a danger—anti-intellectualism on the part of some of us who have our reasons not to be comfortable with the thinking we do. It's not thinking that's the problem—it's what comes of it; I mean, it's what we do with it, how we use it. [You] can't get to be much more of a thinker, an intellectual, a philosopher than Thomas Aquinas; he worked his mind hard so he could understand God's intentions. But today, even our theologians aren't really interested in God—and reading a lot of them, even the most respected, I'm not sure God was really very much in their minds. With all due respect, I'm thinking of your teacher [Paul Tillich]. I hope I'm being clear, and not full of myself, while worrying about a lot of folks these days for being full of their own beliefs, their own ideas. I guess I'm saying that a lot of folks believe in their beliefs, they believe in their ideas, they believe in themselves, and maybe they believe in someone's politics or some social cause: it's today's secularism. I want to add to the brew, here and now, a lot of us churchgoers—this is more complicated and pervasive than those who proclaim their belief in God on one side and those who say 'nothing doing' [with respect to religious faith] on the other side. You can attend church every week, lots of us do, and in your way of thinking, your assumptions as you go through the day, a week—they're essentially secular in nature."

We went on further, substantially longer: an intense conversation with a sincere and devoted Catholic convert who went to church every day, at least during the times I visited him. He'd often sit alone in the local Covington church for a few minutes while I'd sit on the steps outside, and an occasional friend of his, knowing me as his visitor, would say: "Waiting on Dr. Percy?" Meanwhile, (back to Pascal and Weil) he'd be "waiting on God" inside and, afterwards, would be frank to talk about how hard it can be, even in a church, to keep one's mind on "godly matters." "Oh, Walker," I'd often demur, "it's always been that way, from time immemorial—the secular undertow, surely, that existed in the thirteenth century when Aquinas wrote, and surely, as we know directly from Augustine himself, in the fourth century, and again, from Pascal's more personal, self-disclosing pensées, in the seventeenth century: "There are different degrees in this aversion to truth, but all may perhaps be said to have it in some degree, because it is inseparable from self-love." Yes, for sure, Walker agreed—he knew the whole of that one hundredth pensée almost by heart; but there have been "degrees and degrees": some times and places have been, on the whole, more connected to the sacred, some thoroughly or relatively secular.

The "ruins" of his novel *Love in the Ruins* had to do with the consequences of a progressive (in several senses of the word, maybe) secularism: people hopelessly and haplessly adrift, at a thorough remove from one another, and all too confined by their own willing gullibility, the particular train of thought that they find congenial or convincing—each self a sovereignty, and each self out to be as far in the front as possible (with respect to various rank orders, and the devil take the hindmost). Maybe it is, indeed, an ironic conceit (speaking of a secular psychology) to imagine one's own time as more distant from the sacred than other times, more consumed by a worldliness that is not an inevitable experience but a constantly upheld notion of the unqualifiedly desirable. But he was ready to risk the judgment of being blindsided by his own historical moment: yet another would-be visionary who can't quite rise above his own life's (time's) inevitable confinements. "I put the novel [*Love in the Ruins*] in the future, but of course it's only a slight extrapolation from this period we're living in right now to the years ahead that I describe—I'm using a lot of 'symbols,' I suppose you could say, to describe not so much what's coming as what we've already come to! Anyway, whatever I've done—trying to show the 'ruins' of this secular world, so madly adrift, turning here, there, and everywhere for direction, and only half-believing what it decides to hold onto for a while—Flannery O'Connor did it more pointedly in some of her stories. She had it (us!) down cold, what we're like.

"No, I don't think she was finger-pointing—she included herself in her diagnosis of our secular malaise. [I had suggested that she might have risked, at times, a righteousness become self-righteousness, much as I loved her fiction and nonfiction, loved to teach it, too.] I think she's showing you something about yourself, about me, about all of us, if she gets you feeling anxious about her *judgments*, her moral direction, her spiritual 'preoccupations' (that's the way we get back at her, use a word like 'preoccupations' that implies some damn psychiatric disorder!). You bet she's all stirred up—or wants *us* to be! She thinks we're hell-bent, and she wants to say 'fire!' not to create needless panic, but because to her way of thinking (*believing* is the word, I guess!) there *is* a fire, and we'd better take notice! But you know what? There's no danger that she's going to create a big rush to the door, the exit signs, the stairs, with lots of people falling all over each other and some getting hurt or killed. No sir, she knew most people weren't even going to notice—and I mean those 'interleckchuls' she kept parodying. She was trying to tell us what she saw in the mirror and while looking out the window—both. Somehow, she managed to get herself out of the world around her enough to give her distance on things. I tried to get that distance by pushing things hard, exaggerating a little, by saying to the reader (to myself, first): hey, look where we're going; look where we're headed—from here to there, that's where we'll be, any minute now! But Flannery didn't have to go to that kind of 'extreme.' She almost went 'back,' if anything! She took the reader into the 'earlier' time of those country scenes, with country people—and boy, what she let us know, *see*, that way!"

Of the thirty-one stories in Flannery O'Connor's *Complete Stories*, "The Artificial Nigger" was reportedly one of her favorites, maybe *the* favorite. It is a story all too easy to summarize. A sixty-year-old grandfather named Mr. Head takes his ten-year-old grandson, Nelson, by train from their backwoods home to the big city, where with a great show of self-assurance the older man plays learned guide and instructor to the innocent child. On the train, and down the strange urban streets, the saga unfolds—the supposedly wise, experienced teacher constantly pressing his knowledge on a young one both eager to learn and also intuitively aware that he is, most significantly, a foil for his grandfather's cocksure sense of himself: the know-it-all anxious to lord it over a companion who is expected to register awe and gratitude at every turn of this voyage of initiation and discovery. The story's dramatic high point takes place in a back alley of the big city. Nelson, tired as can be, has dozed off. The grandfather, worried lest they miss the train back home, awakens him with a "loud noise by banging his foot against the [garbage] can." The boy is roused all right, lurches forward "like a wild maddened pony." Soon enough he has knocked down a lady, who claims a broken ankle, calls for the police, attracts a crowd. The grandfather has cautiously trailed Nelson, is there as the boy is surrounded by un-friendly people who are awaiting the arrival of the po-lice. Under those circumstances—the critical moment in the story—the grandfather, with the suggestive name of Head, denies any connection to the boy: "This is not my boy," and further, "I never seen him before." The rest of the story has to do with the eventual, guarded reconciliation of the two: they wander about, near one another physically, but at an utter remove psychologi-cally and spiritually. They stumble, however, into a "plaster figure of a Negro sitting bent over on a low yel-low brick fence that curved around a wide lawn." In an instant, the lost pair of wanderers, estranged from one another, make common cause, as it were, with the plas-ter figure: "They stood gazing at the artificial Negro as if they were faced with some great mystery, some monu-ment to another's victory that brought them together in their common defeat." The two have happened upon "an action of mercy" and soon enough are on their way home.

Such a summary does scant justice to an allegorical narrative that is, really, in the tradition of *Pilgrim's Progress*. It is no accident, of course, that the story's pro-tagonist is named Mr. Head, and that at the very end of the story the train which has carried them to and from the city is likened to "a serpent in the woods." Nor are O'Connor's references to light and darkness without major implication: at the start of what turns out to be a "moral mission" a "coarse-looking orange sun" appears, but in no time the two are "lost," as in *Paradise Lost*, and a heavy darkness has settled over them—to be replaced, at the end, upon their cautious, wary reconciliation, by a "moon restored to its full splendor," one that "sprang from a cloud and flooded the clearing with light."

This densely symbolic story is accessible, sustained by the down-home dialect of ordinary Southern folk whose way of putting things Miss O'Connor knew cold. In truth, the story tells of the humbling of Head—of a confident worldly Intellect (so the boy Nelson was forcefully persuaded to believe) become quite something else. At the beginning we are given the Enlightenment (though the author tips her hand, somewhat, by describing that sun as "coarse-looking," a forecast of the coarse behavior to come). For a while the callow youth learns from the ever so knowledgeable elder. What is learned has to do with human affairs, with race and class. Nelson is asked questions by his teacher, who is only too glad to correct the boy, point out his ignorance, his inadequate grasp of the reality they are jointly encountering. Again and again we are witness to the condescensions of a heady one: Mr. Head determined to exact a compliant, awestruck respect from a Nelson who is being told things but also being told off when he expresses the least doubt or misgivings, or when he displays a natural curiosity that unnerves his supposedly all-knowing mentor, a would-be intellectual authority of the first order.

At one point, in a brief exchange, Miss O'Connor manages with brilliant precision a vividly compelling, probing examination of the origins of racism: ten or twenty textbooks of social science get packed into a few

fictional lines. Nelson is being queried by his patronizing grandfather Head about "a huge coffee-colored
man" who had passed them on the train on their way
cityward. The boy doesn't give quite the answer his
teacher wants—he calls the man "fat" and "old." Finally, his teacher, having had enough, declares, "That
was a nigger"; he does so with a smug self-satisfaction
and rubs it in by remarking to a "man across the aisle"
that the person just discussed was the boy's "first
nigger." A fellow human being has now become the occasion of a child's gratuitous humiliation. The boy is
angry but can hardly turn on his powerful grandfather-
guide, who has just made matters very much worse by
calling the lad ignorant, and even moving to another
seat across the aisle—a moment that portends the
story's central thrust, that of human "alienation" as a
consequence of human pride.

What choice, then, for this boy, needlessly humiliated by his own kin now become a vain, self-exalting
"expert," all too sure of himself and all too pretentiously
insistent on letting his "pupil" learn, unforgettably,
who knows more than whom? "Nelson turned backward again and looked where the Negro had disap-
peared," our authorial voice tells us—and then another
"turn," this one within the child's mind: "He felt that
the Negro had deliberately walked down the aisle in
order to make a fool of him and he hated him with a
fierce raw hate; and also he understood why his grandfather disliked them." Now a youngster who has been
fighting for a modicum of self-respect from the over-
bearing Head is ready to surrender, be the apt, atten-
tive, submissive learner. Now, as today's psychology

would put it, abstractly, an "identification with the aggressor" has taken place—at a high cost, though: a boy's felt inadequacy and vulnerability has prompted him to find a scapegoat, one readily available in the "coffee-colored man" whom he originally had the innocent decency to regard as "a man," then as "a fat man," then as "an old man." Now, hustled and intimidated and cajoled and seduced by Head, the boy is ready to join the adult world; he is, as the contemporary language of psychology would have it, "socialized." Pain and self-doubt have become transmuted into hate—a grim kind of "education."

In the end Miss O'Connor offers her lesson: the democracy of misery. Now we have seen, yet again, that pride goeth before the fall. Now an intellectual arrogance has prompted an edgy distrust in this pair of blood relatives. They are estranged, confused—again, lost. Soon enough (as in the story of Christ), the young person is denied, by his grandfather and teacher, no less; and soon enough, the two, their bond seemingly sundered beyond any hope of repair, wander in the desert ("Here everything was deserted"). Yet grace will shine upon them—unexpectedly, by its very definition: a mere piece of plaster, a silly reminder of human folly and ignorance and, yes, mean-spirited arrogance offers a redemptive moment for these two troubled souls, each so alone, one through bitter disappointment, the other through a deep-down sense of his failure as a teacher, his willingness, in the clutch, to betray his grandson, rather than endure the disapproval of a crowd. The quiet resonance of this story with that of Christ, and, too, that of Dietrich Bonhoeffer, say, in this century, is all too clear, and intentional. Who deserts whom, and when and why? Who stands up for what, when, and for which reasons? The very disciples of Jesus had left his side at the end: yet another mob able to put even the morally awake into a deep sleep. As for the Christian clergy of Hitler's Germany, they truckled under overwhelmingly to the hordes Hitler so handily mobilized—with Bonhoeffer, as a consequence, very much alone at the end of his life's determined and unyielding moral vigil.

As Dr. Percy wanted me to remember, Flannery O'Connor constructed a short fiction that took sharp aim at the twentieth-century secular world she had observed so closely. She gave us our secularity, as she openly acknowledged, from a particular vantage point: "I see from the standpoint of Christian orthodoxy. This means for me that the meaning of life is centered in our Redemption by Christ, and what I see in the world I see in relation to that Christ." She was, thereby, spelling out a sacred angle of vision as hers; and so, over and over, she confounds us secular readers, who may admire her talent, her skills as a writer, her sharply astute capacity to spot pretense, hypocrisy, and, most of all, self-importance, and, in no time, mock them into an unnerving exposure—often to our discomfort, because we ourselves, late-twentieth-century secularists, are precisely the ones being portrayed by a writer who as a youth was a cartoonist, and who never lost an ability for caricature.

In the O'Connor canon, the sacred is almost beyond recognition, whereas the secular, in all its obvious triumph, is a heap of transparent, rote clichés, banalities.

In one of her best-known stories, "A Good Man Is Hard to Find," a serial killer (the Misfit) is on the loose while an American family journeys south on a vacation. Sure enough, the Misfit comes upon them and especially confronts the most senior member of the family, an elderly grandmother, presumably the repository (as with Mr. Head) of whatever wisdom is available. She tries ever so hard to "understand" this violent outsider, wants to pray for him and somehow heal him, but he is beyond her reach. He will continue on his rampage; and the reader doesn't know what to do: the grandmother's pieties ring false but tell us so much about the shallowness of the American moral landscape, as portrayed, at least, by one observer of it—whereas the Misfit's arbitrary murderousness is, of course, beyond all comprehension. Miss O'Connor has harkened back to Christ's terribly confounding and unsettling mix of explanation and warning: "I come to bring you not peace, but the sword." Yet again, that Georgian lady, even as she struggled with the devastations of a mortal illness, disseminated lupus (the very name a jolt to the imagination), was determined to strip us lean, morally: her convictions with respect to the sacred brought to bear with a mercilessly exact aim on our secular way of thinking.

In one story after another, in "Good Country People" and in "The Enduring Chill" and in "The Lame Shall Enter First," the central figure of the fictional struggle, the one who embodies our present-day values and expectations and sympathies and loyalties, the one with whom we are tempted to agree, and identify, is revealed as deeply flawed morally; in each instance it is a matter of a prideful intellect that serves its owner poorly, makes him or her all too self-absorbed and in-different to others, even those close by virtue of membership in the same family. As she works that theme over, O'Connor probes what I suppose might be called a secular progression of sorts, a "developmental psychology," a series of "moral stages," though she would surely shun such social science talk. Still, she had keen eyes and ears, had taken the measure of our days, ways, hence her analysis of how the secular mind, here and now, works.

In the beginning, she reminds us, there are the minds eager to know, anxious to expand their awareness. These are individuals who are sure of themselves as teachers or thinkers, as aspiring writers or scholars or healers: people who are quick to think of themselves as more advanced intellectually than others, and with some justification. They have gone to school, college, graduate school; or they have broken with the customs of other less worthy folks around them, the ignorant or the superstitious, or, yes, the narrow and bigoted—and so they are in the vanguard of thought, as compared with their neighbors. They may be older, have had a good deal of sobering experience in life, and therefore with some obvious justification feel themselves a leg up on certain others. Finally, they are men and women who are natively intuitive, or have been lucky enough to learn about the world through travel, and consequently are sometimes able to distance themselves from the all too apparent narrowness, even blindness, and assuredly the ignorance of those nearby in one or another town. Here, after a fashion, is O'Connor's version of the long-heralded and, these days, much vaunted "New South":

those who, with great satisfaction and with conviction and with no little sense of personal worth, are intent on leading a region long held by others, from afar, to be benighted into a contemporary, secular "promised land." In that new Canaan money flows more widely across a long impoverished land, and, too, schools and colleges take on great meaning, and cultural pursuits (museums, orchestras, galleries, bookstores, theaters) all prosper, as do universities devoted to turning out educated businessmen, engineers, doctors, and lawyers, and, not least, future professors. All of that O'Connor attends and evokes, sometimes in a wickedly seductive and ultimately provocative (even enraging) manner: she will "build up" her assortment of artists, psychotherapists, university graduates with advanced degrees, and individuals with advanced ideas, people eager to bid good-bye to the South's racial segregation, its formerly intransigent caste system, in favor of professed "interest" in the blacks, a readiness to see them, at the least, as fellow voters, as classmates of their own kin in schools, as sharers of buses, of seats at movie houses and in restaurants—all quite promising, quite "progressive."

Yet, soon enough, this congenial expression of bright prospects yields to quite something else: an ambition for intellectual advancement, for social change, for a heightened awareness become, in their sum, a source of pride in the sense of achievements celebrated, but also in the (biblical) sense of a smugness, a congratulatory self-regard that soars. Now, hope turns to expectation—everything, in time, will be known. Science is not only a many splendored thing; it is the eventual victor in any and all confrontations with nature, with ourselves as a big part of nature, hence O'Connor's wry remark once that "mystery is a great embarrassment to the modern mind." Give us but time, and the funding, and we will clear aside those mysteries, we say or hear others say, in laboratories and classrooms, and outside them, too—a shared public notion, if not fantasy.

Meanwhile, as Erik H. Erikson observed in connection with psychoanalysis, idolatry and insistent or even punitive orthodoxy are not incompatible with such "progress" in the mind's mastery of itself and its surroundings. To repeat, Freud, ridiculing the "illusion" of religious faith, himself became an object of veneration for many, at least for a while, his every word given more credibility than he himself may have thought possible or desirable: Freudianism. Marx, similarly contemptuous of religion, became a historical figure whose picture was waved in Red Square. And in the "dictatorship of the proletariat," Stalin's rule, and other all too grim, even murderous, reminders of the way in which what got proudly called "scientific materialism" (the heart of secular thinking) became, in fact, brute and blind statism, a faith all its own imposed through relentlessly enforced indoctrination: from reflection in the name of the mind's independence to propaganda as an instrument of compulsory mass persuasion. Indeed, those of us who have done documentary work, used words and photographs and film footage to render, we hope accurately, compassionately, sensitively, and sensibly, the lives of others, have other kinds of "documentary" efforts to contemplate, lest we, also, become all too taken with our capacities, our sense of what we have done and can do and hope to do: Leni Riefenstahl's *Triumph of*

the Will, of course, but no less notorious, if less powerfully effective, the mobilization of writing and photog-
raphy that advanced the interests of Nazi and Soviet political and intellectual and cultural hegemony. (Not
that, in more subtle or indirect ways, of course, any political and economic system, including a capitalist one,
a democratic one, doesn't exert, in some degree, a shaping influence on its own citizens through the verbal and
visual messages sent to them by those who own television companies, newspapers, magazines, movie studios,
publishing houses.)

When Flannery O'Connor remarked that "the task
of the novelist is to deepen mystery," she was, needless
to say, throwing down the gauntlet to a fact-obsessed
world; and on a so-called higher level, she was challenging a theory-committed world in which those facts are
assembled to suit the conveniences and purposes of various concepts and the conceptualists who have promul-
gated them. She saw us as ever intent on proving ourselves aware of, and in progressive or potential control
of, all things, and, she believed, ironically unaware of
the consequences of such an outlook. True, there are, as
the clichéd language of today has it, "problems" and "issues" to be (that cool, slippery word) "resolved," so any
of us social scientists can be overheard admitting. But
the prominent secular modes of thought, no matter
their dark or dour sides, emphasize an eventual upbeat
outcome—the reason, perhaps, for their "success": an
embrace from a here-and-now world that worries not
about Armageddon, expects not a Judgment Day, hopes
not for a Heaven, fears not a Hell, but for sure counts
hard and bets everything on a longer and better spell of

it in this place of ours. The dream was that the heartless exploitation of the working class would give way to a world in which the state "withered away." The dream was that a searching acknowledgment of our lusts and rivalries would, through the pursuit of psychoanalysis by more and more individuals, give us a clearheaded citizenry. The dream was that physicists and biologists, their minds brilliantly set on exploring the minutest details of matter, would end up doing so all right, to the point that human life would last and last, a huge span of time at our beck and call. Nor is such optimism, today, in jeopardy, some disappointments notwithstanding. Good cheer about what we can do, what the consequence of what we do will turn out to be, is a hallmark of our time. Economists will steer us through, and psychologists, and chemists and computer technologists and research physicians, and research engineers: our "down" side will be explored and, over the generations, will recede, a consequence of (scientific) light over the murky, darker elements in this life.

For O'Connor, of course, the "mystery" to which she referred is not a matter of luck, good and bad, or of our uncertain capacity to weather unexpected obstacles put in our way by fate; she knew the mystery of evil, as well—of human "finitude," of the limits of imagination and thoughtfulness, and, very important, of reason itself, since it is something that will always emerge from our necessarily flawed minds (so she believed them to be). Put differently, she believed in God's mysteries and, with them, in the Devil, that fallen angel who nevertheless (in her eyes) has had a continuing existence, across all generations. She was not morbid, but she was not naive, and she had excellent moral vision, as attested by stories such as "The Displaced Person" and "Everything That Rises Must Converge": both of them take direct aim at various secular anticipations, at our confidence in who or what we are, at the silver lining we always find—if not the pie in the sky—as we contemplate even our troubling social reality, or the less than attractive personal qualities any of us can be found possessing. For her, an obvious irony is around the corner of any moment of achieved or fortuitous benevolence, the devil always having slippery shoes. To Freud's maxim, in the name of explorative science, that the Id's greed and tumult will give way to the Ego's confident, penetratingly effective knowledge (all wielded for the good), she would, no doubt, pose a historian's account of recent times, not to mention the observations of us made by various philosophers, theologians, novelists, poets. Surely, she'd align herself with the physicist Pascal (as in his "law of pressure"), who, like her, died at only thirty-nine, but who found time to give us this mention of the Ego, under the classificatory title of "self-love" (in his one hundredth pensée):

> The nature of self-love and of this human Ego is to love self only and consider self only. But what will man do? He cannot prevent this object that he loves from being full of faults and wants. He wants to be great and he sees himself small. He wants to be happy, and he sees himself miserable. He wants to be perfect, and he sees himself full of imperfection. He wants to be the object of love and esteem among men, and he sees that his faults merit only their hatred and contempt. This

embarrassment in which he finds himself produces in him the most unrighteous and criminal passion that can be imagined; for he conceives a mortal enmity against that truth which reproves him, and which convinces him of his faults.

Here, for Pascal, was the psychological essence of the secular mind. Even in the grim Marx, the gloomy realist Freud, the trembling experimental physicist or biologist, worried sick about what *might* happen to us, courtesy of nuclear proliferation or the emergence of new and deadly bacterial strains or viruses, there is the feisty and proud fighter who says no to such a "downer" as Pascal's comment—as he himself well knew:

> He [we] would annihilate it [such a recognition of our "human Ego" as has just been described], but, unable to destroy it in its essence, he [meaning, any of us] destroys it as far as possible in his own knowledge and in that of others; that is to say, he devotes all his attention to hiding his faults both from others and from himself, and he cannot endure either that others should point them out to him, or that he should see them. Truly it is an evil to be full of faults; but it is still greater evil to be full of them and to be unwilling to recognize them, since that is to add the further fault of a voluntary illusion.

A surprising, if not stunning intellectual irony: Pascal, in the name of Christian (sacred) realism, anticipated Freud's secular realism—and then some. It is as if Blaise in the seventeenth century said to Sigmund in the twentieth: look, my dear friend, I appreciate fully (heartily, too) your desire to plumb the depths, get to the bottom of things, dispel all possible illusions; I only worry about your own. A self-described conquistador who has earned title to the word, you make the mistake of confusing particular battles with a war—no, the metaphor fails here: with, rather, a *condition*, something that *is*. I know that mention of such a notion goes against every grain of your thought. For you (as for me) the mind is full of the egoism, the narcissism you and your followers call it, that we both have explored. We differ, though, on what is possible in the future, in *any* future. For you there is knowledge as the ultimate winner, despite that narcissism, and its discontents, its dangers—if not psychoanalysis, then biochemistry, and if not that, then some other unforeseeable, triumphant turn of the scientific (i.e., secular) screw. For me, there is our human situation as it has been handed down to us from on high (forgive me if I become slyly ambiguous here, a doubter's privilege as he struggles, even so, for faith), meaning from God, or God as Nature (as part of Himself, Herself, Itself, whatever!).

You will laugh, my colleague, and say that such a viewpoint makes you, a proudly skeptical and cautious pessimist, seem positively utopian in outlook, but I must continue with this. For you secularists there is always possibility; that is, your faith in the mind's Promethean exertions and their subsequent achievements. For us, in contrast, who are secularists as well, but who strive toward the sacred, check in with it, so to speak, constantly and urgently, slouching (rather than striding) toward Jerusalem, as the poet has said of us, there is only so much possibility, because there is, as well, a certain bedrock finality to who we are, to what we seek and contend with. Round and round versions of us go, get regarded and defined (different words at different times), but in a rock-bottom sense our nature is *there*, as it has always been. We leap ahead, yes, of course, but so doing, we also return to certain inevitable and utterly fundamental qualities, situations: love and its discontents, including the "self-love" we have both discussed at such (knowing!) length; the various psychological and moral and social vulnerabilities of this life; ambition and resolve and conviction and fear and resentment and envy and jealousy and hate, and, finally, the knowledge that somehow, someway, sometime, no matter the other knowledge that has held it at bay, death will bring us to the end of this stay. That knowledge, our awareness of death, goes to the heart of our unyielding (you abhor the word, I know) humanity: an existentialism, that is, finally, in certain important respects, unalterable in its character, our illusions notwithstanding—those that go under the name of science and progress, rather than religion, meaning those that are secular rather than tied to the sacred.

IV

Where We Are Headed

WE IN the Western bourgeois world are committed, as mentioned, to the future, resolutely and consistently so. That slant, toward what is coming rather than what has been, is itself an important attribute of the secular mind. Why turn back and imagine what Pascal might have to say, based on what he has already so tellingly said, were he with us now (and especially if he wasn't, back then, a hopeful visionary with great expectations galore), when we can make prophets of ourselves, or by association, as eager, willing (sometimes, decidedly gullible) readers, part of a collective farsighted response: a culture of upbeat anticipation? Poor Pascal, anyway—so "depressed," so in need of Prozac, so immersed in the tortures (the self-torture) of an accusatory Catholicism worthy, actually, of some of the frenzied Puritan divines who began to settle America around the time he was being so "hard" on himself, not to mention the rest of us! Instead, we wear our binoculars, scan the coming years, extrapolate from what now is to what, for sure, will be, go further, give ourselves permission to run way ahead, down through more than the decades.

One such look ahead was ironically titled *Looking Backward*—Edward Bellamy's fictional effort in 1888 to envision the America of our time. He gives us a Boston both flourishing and fair-minded, the proverbial "city on the hill" of its Puritan forebears realized at last in the year 2000. He gives us a socialism that is appealing, vibrant: an egalitarian world that is a telling contrast to the Gilded Age. Now, at the start of a new millennium, the America that Henry George described in *Progress and Poverty* (1879) had given way to a country of bustling cities and towns all of whose inhabitants lived comfortable and connected lives.

When Bellamy's central character, Julian West, wakes up, scans the business and cultural life of Boston and beyond, he has sailed during his long sleep across a century and more of strife and injustice, landed safe and well on the shores of a "promised land"—with electricity and credit cards and shopping malls and a version of the radio: a novelist's uncanny capacity to imagine predictively a strikingly different life from the one he observed daily. But Bellamy's utopian story, so often hailed for the accuracy of its depiction of our contemporary habits and gadgetry, is really a moral and psychological fantasy, an idea of a nation whose citizens are kindly, contemplative, courteous, and, above all, uninterested in grabbing all they can get, no matter the consequences for others. Bellamy believed us Americans to be perfectible within, even as he saw us becoming rich; he portrays us as both just and tolerant. For him, our great lust would be for benevolence: our idealism wouldn't be deterred; our minds and hearts would flourish under such circumstances. Here is a civilized, humane Superego, well able to tame judiciously the now attenuated and discreet pressures of the Id, and an Ego free ("free at last") to pursue virtues as well as property. Meanwhile (the irony!) we, who live in the America Bellamy foretold, find *ourselves* "looking backward," making all too suggestive and melancholy comparisons between the economic and social disparities of the late nineteenth century and those of our time.

To be sure, not all futurist fantasies have been confidently joyful hymns to our dreams become a realized series of breakthroughs. In the darkest hours of this century and, maybe, of all centuries, only fifty years ago, George Orwell, in 1948, gave us his well-known *1984*. There he called a halt to the Ego—the one George Eliot and Sir Willoughby in their different ways knew, the one Pascal and Freud knew, the one Pascal thought would always be, or the one Freud thought might well one day emerge. Dorothea's "theoretic" mind in *Middlemarch*, Sir Willoughby's endlessly vain mind in *The Egoist*, Pascal's portrayal of an Ego also quite self-preoccupied, though with no true conviction of its ultimate virtue, quite the contrary, and Freud's portrayal of an Ego buffeted, but also potentially capable of taking matters into its own hands (taking its owner, after all, to see a psychoanalyst: will as the Ego's great instrument of assertion, no matter an Id that resembles Pascal's description of a side of us)—all of that, in Orwell's premonitory chronicle, becomes almost irrelevant. For the time was approaching (only thirty-six years ahead, a couple of generations at the most) when the Ego as rendered by all four of those writers, two novelists, two scientists with speculative tendencies, would be mere putty in the hands of something larger than any human being, something with a momentum of its own, a strangely impersonal (and inhuman) construction of social and political reality that would have enormous, compelling, even definitive sway over all within its grasp. In essence, Orwell gave us an Ego strangely placid, imperturbable, no longer pressed by Freud's Id, no longer troubled within by Pascal's moral misgivings, no longer swollen by Meredith's version of unembarrassed conceit or Eliot's of heedless self-regard (theoretical elaboration as a variant of self-promotion), but now the property of something else: the state's (moral, political) power become for the individual a commanding and pervasive presence—the Ego as something *without*, enforcing its institutional will on the within of all those subjugated "mass-men" (Czeslaw Milosz's "captive mind").

We breathe easier these days, surely. Orwell's apprehension has not quite come true—that more and more totalitarian states would control not only the civic life of their subjects, or their economic fate, or the cultural values given expression, but their minds in a more direct and intimate way: what they think, the language they use, how they speak to one another. Of course, many of us in the social sciences and in psychoanalytic psychiatry have, perhaps, underestimated all along the impact on individuals of all that happens in the name of race, class, politics, culture as it affirms itself on the radio, on television, on the Internet, in journalism, in advertising, in the theater. It took me some time, in the course of working with children caught in political and social and racial crises, to realize that their mental life had to do not only with the relationships they had with their mothers and fathers and brothers and sisters, but with the larger world they inhabited. All the time children's thoughts and impressions and opinions and concerns and misgivings and fears are being shaped outside their homes as well as within them: in neighborhoods, and in the realm that reaches them through the television set or on-line, or as they sit watching a movie in the living room or a theater. Yet with Stalinism gone, with the terrible likes of Hitler a constantly receding nightmare, with democracies increasingly prevalent in our own hemisphere, we can assure ourselves that the "brainwashing" so often described in earlier decades of this century, and so vividly evoked, satirized by Orwell, is no longer a threat to us.

Yet Orwell may have been more pervasively and broadly prophetic than we want him to be; he may well have meant to examine across the board the nature of political and of cultural authority, their influence on a nation's citizens, and to do so as a satirist does, through the exaggerations of caricature. After all, during the Second World War he worked for the BBC; he was no stranger, then, to politics become public "information," if not outright propaganda. (The latter, of course, is always what one's enemies describe; the former what one's own side is trying to get across.) In any event, Orwell was at pains, apart from *1984*, to remind us that the language we use, the reading we favor, and what we are taught to make of that reading, has to do with a lot more than the emergence of Fascism or Communism, with their statist encroachment on private life. In "Boys' Weeklies," in "Politics vs. Literature," in "Poetry and the Microphone," in "Notes on Nationalism," in "The Prevention of Literature," he kept taking on "culture" and "political power" as they bear down on our ways of thinking, our minds. For him "the huge bureaucratic machines" that he mentions in "Poetry and the Microphone" (it was published in 1945, well before *1984* appeared) exert enormous psychological impact on our personal lives and become, in fact, overseers, even as they control so many of us, economically, politically. For him, too, Freud's Superego was not merely a consequence of family life, a "construct" that we theorists invoke as a means of referring to countless admonitions by mothers and fathers become, eventually, a child's notion of ought and naught, probably yes and definitely no. Rather, parents and children alike learn to shape their sense of the possible, the desirable, the forbidden in response to a host of institutional imperatives quite evidently and concretely transmitted to them, to all of us. A novelist rather than a theorist, Orwell nevertheless extended the psychoanalytic paradigm for widespread public consideration. In truth, he intuitively sensed what the young Willhelm Reich had noted in his work on "character types," that the mind responds significantly to the social forces of a society as well as the particular "dynamics" of this or that family, and he had also anticipated by several years Erik H. Erikson's similar line of reasoning in *Childhood and Society* (1950).

Orwell, the idiosyncratic, levelheaded agnostic and skeptic, was crankily contemptuous of "principalities and powers," including his own socialist brethren. He looked askance at the modern state, and the corporate world, and, especially, the media—so much under the control of one or the other of those two. But his picture of the future was based on gloomy conjecture rather than on substantial experience. In contrast, Milosz's *The Captive Mind* draws on a prophetic poet's daily contact with a Stalinism terribly triumphant after the Second World War. Indeed, only five years after *1984* was published, Milosz would make this crucial comparative observation in *The Captive Mind*:

> The citizen of the people's democracies is immune to the kind of neurosis that takes such manifold forms in capitalist countries. In the West, a man subconsciously regards society as unrelated to him. Society indicates the limits he must not exceed; in exchange for this he receives a guarantee that no one will meddle excessively in his affairs. If he loses it's his own fault; let psychoanalysis help him. In the East there is no boundary between man and society. His game, and whether he loses or wins, is a public matter. He is never alone. If he loses it is *not* because of indifference on the part of his environment, but because the environment keeps him under such minute scrutiny. Neuroses as they are known in the West result, above all, from man's aloofness; so even if they were allowed to practice, psychoanalysts would not earn a plum, in the people's democracies.

Here categorical assertion, even in supremely sensitive and accomplished hands, proves as inadequate as futurist fiction, such as *1984*. It is worth noting, however, that Orwell the polemical essayist (and, during the Second World War, unashamed propagandist for Great Britain, no matter his egalitarian misgivings) was shrewdly unwilling to engage in the kind of unqualified analysis that tempts Milosz in the above statement, whose simplifications, however, bear their own story:

the scarcely suppressed anxiety and anger of a private person who sees firsthand and everywhere the monolithic state "moving in," stifling any and all expressions of particular souls in favor of the rehearsed slogans, exhortative always, of officialdom. We in the West, now, have the privilege of noticing, right off, and in comfortable retrospect, the exaggerations of such a midcentury description of what Churchill's "fall of the iron curtain" meant for the psychology of millions. We can, with justification, remind ourselves repeatedly that we, too, are not immune to the strong, if less explicit and uniformed and politically engineered, influences abroad in our respective (capitalist, democratic) lands. Still, for Milosz the quantitative had become qualitative, and he surely had every right to worry: a secular, political Superego hugely watchful, able to exact a good deal of compliance from the instinctual life of a people, and able to command from the Ego every bit of responsive adherence, at first perhaps out of an edgy, reluctant awareness of *realpolitik*, and, eventually, with the unwilling, reflexic alacrity of true "indoctrination"—so the parents of Milosz's age must have worriedly foreseen as their children's fate, or that of their children's children. How long, Milosz must have wondered, would his fellow Polish citizens stay even remotely loyal in their heads and hearts, never mind their Sunday habits, to the Catholic Church, in the face of the overwhelming presence of a totalitarian regime in their lives, its authority everywhere in evidence: on the radio and television, in the newspapers and magazines, in the schools and universities, on constant public display through well-organized parades, through the sight, all the time, of the police, the army, the hovering helicopters and zooming bombers and fighters of the air force?

We know decades later that Orwell's fictional nightmare, and that of Milosz (based, again, on experience, on direct observation rather than futurist alarm) have not come to pass—a function of a political and religious struggle fought successfully in Europe and elsewhere. History is more complex than the dramatic temptations of a novelist such as Orwell permit, especially when the novelist (not unlike some of us social scientists) wants to make a provocative, singular point. Nevertheless, Milosz's sober conclusions were drawn from his acute awareness of what was, at a minimum, in the process of taking place, no matter its eventual outcome. Moreover, many thousands must have, at least partially, fallen victim to what he described, their lives witness to the psychological realization of what Orwell could only render in apprehensive speculation. Again, it was back, in Eastern Europe, a matter of degree, a struggle being waged; and no doubt about it, one has to keep insisting, the same situation of a merely *relative* independence of thought and feeling (with respect to various social and political structures) applies to our lives in the West. How significantly, as a matter of fact, did the Catholic Church influence the minds of its faithful in Poland (or elsewhere) eighty years ago, sixty years ago, never mind during the decades when commissars took on cardinals unto death for the minds (souls) of a nation's, a continent's population? Why did both Orwell and Milosz seriously underestimate the sacred as they took measure of the secular—in East and West alike? The pope's visit to Cuba, his enthusiastic reception there, tells us, yet again, of the limits of the secular, no matter its might, even as the sacred must contend constantly with secular intrusions.

In this regard, I return in my memory to a conversation I had in 1973 with Dorothy Day, in her living quarters at the Catholic Workers' St. Joseph's House, at 36 East First Street in New York City. She was reminiscing about her earlier life as a suffragette, as an ardent secular person who lived in Greenwich Village, wrote for the socialist paper *The Call,* embraced various "causes" of the time, the 1920s. Her life had changed after she gave birth to her daughter Tamar (the child of a friendship rather than a marriage): a subsequent conversion to the Catholic Church, to which she thereafter gave herself fully in mind and heart. Yet she was ever the astute observer of others, of herself, and as the author of a novel and a screenplay or two, she had trouble ignoring human complexity, paradox, inconsistency. After singing the praises of a church's traditions and values, which she didn't hesitate to describe as nothing short of "lifesaving" in their impact on her, she suddenly shifted her point of view, and with a furrowed brow offered these words: "I love sitting in church praying. I try not to let it be automatic—I try to be myself and talk to God as honestly and spontaneously as I can. I'm afraid—I'm really afraid that going to church and praying will become an automatic thing with me. I'm afraid I'll be going through the motions—that I won't be thinking, or be *myself* praying—that I'll be half conscious, daydreaming. I'm in church seeking the sacred, but I go there as a secular person. I feel split, try as I might not to be!

"I told the priest all of this [what she had at some great length been telling me, of which the above is but a part] and he wasn't happy with what I said! He reprimanded me! He said I hadn't yet learned to be a 'natural Catholic.' He said the church should be a 'regular' part of your life—you shouldn't be thinking too much about it, and be 'self-conscious' about it. Well, I wasn't ready to surrender so fast! I said, 'Father, yes, I see what you mean. But how about just 'conscious,' not 'self-conscious,' but 'conscious'? He wasn't pleased with me at all! He said he was afraid that my definition of 'conscious' is his of 'self-conscious.' He said the church has its own ways of influencing your life, and you shouldn't hold it up to secular standards—the sacred gets to you 'slow time,' and the secular 'fast time,' right away. He said I'm trying to 'force' things in church!

"I didn't want to talk with him much more about this! Maybe I'll never be able to be the 'regular' or 'natural' Catholic he wants me to be—or maybe I'll never forget what happened to some of my dear friends who became Communists [in the 1930s]. I'm not here to 'red-bait,' I never did. I could see then, and I *still* can, why they chose as they did. But I saw their minds get swept up, swept away. They criticized people for getting swept up by capitalist materialism, and then they got swept up by another kind of materialism. They seemed to lose all their independence; they said what they were supposed to say—I would be talking to them, and I could almost predict, word for word, what I'd hear coming out of their mouths! It was scary to me—not that I would necessarily disagree with what they were trying to get at. It was the *automatic* way they spoke, the instant replies, with the words and phrases I'd been hearing for years. I recall one of my friends speaking like that—I recall thinking afterwards: he's lost, his mind is gone; it's no longer his mind, it belongs to the party, and its spokesmen, and to what's decided by them, the higher-ups, here and abroad. I'm not talking about 'discipline,' here; I'm talking about believing something, the faith that you must take your orders in what you say or do, that you aren't really responsible for anything on your own, but only as part of something larger, called Communism, and your life is to be put on the line for that [ideology], in a manner that others decide, and you're in a holding pattern: you wait for those others to tell you what to do.

"I don't say it's not the same, being a Catholic, or for that matter, a devout Protestant or Jew. I'm just saying that anything is possible for any of us, that we can take religion or politics or some set of ideas, and end up living in such a way that we lose all sense of who we are— our minds no longer belong to us. I know, I know— that is what some passionate religious pilgrims say they are *hoping* will happen to them! [I had suggested as much.] But I'm hoping it's not completely the same— because God isn't here, whereas Lenin and Stalin and all those who speak in their name are very much one of us flawed, sinful human beings. I know, yes, the bishops and cardinals, the priests and nuns, are 'flawed, sinful human beings,' too. [I had made mention of that obvious point.] But God isn't that—it's the heart of the religious faith, to believe so. You know, when people ask me why I converted, *that's* what I tell them, that I was looking for something beyond this secular life, that I've lived to the full, I'll have to admit, and I found that something in a sacred tradition, and so when I go to church, I try to *live* my religion, *live* that sacred time in that sacred place, and that's what I was trying to tell the priest the other day: I get frightened I'll pick up my old secular ways in church and, while praying, just go through the motions the way I used to, when I was living in the Village and going fast, fast—always something to do, or some new idea to have, or people to meet."

She stopped, and seemed elsewhere in her thoughts, maybe visiting yet again that "secular life" to which she had just referred. I was finally beginning to understand what she had been trying to tell me—about the struggle on her part to be a believing, loyal, faithful Catholic, but not an "automatic" one. She wanted to be a believer whose *will* was part of her faith; whose *intellect* was also part of her faith; whose *passions* even, were part of her faith. She wanted, put differently, her very own, personal sacred life: her particular mix of desire (Id) and conscience (Superego) as they are handled by her "consciousness," the word she kept having in mind as she conversed with the priest, a version of Freud's Ego. She feared a surrender of her mind not to spiritual faith but to institutional authority, even as she very much felt connected to that institution's authority. It was a real tightrope she was walking, but one she very much wanted (willed, contemplated) to walk. Hers, I dared surmise, but not say, was a struggle to be a devout Catholic believer whose faith was *hers*, hers to give, as opposed to a Catholic believer who had lost a sense of herself as the one who offered her faith upward, as it were.

Again, an elusive distinction, perhaps, and one subject to interpretations (theological, creedal, psychoanalytic) other than the kind I knew then, and now, to make. Still, in her own way, I thought then, and do now, she was addressing matters that Orwell and Arthur Koestler (in *Darkness at Noon*, a book Milosz mentions in his *Captive Mind*) also struggled to comprehend. How to hold secure one's own moral and spiritual self, one's personal, reflective destiny—amidst the crushing institutional forces of the state, but also of the marketplace and, yes, the church in its decidedly secular aspect?

In the world of George Eliot and Meredith, and Freud, too, the Ego is buffeted by the ever demanding Id and a Superego of varying sway, depending on the particular person in question. None of Eliot's fictional individuals nor Meredith's are overwhelmed by a punitive conscience. Indeed, even Dostoievsky's obsessed characters, such as Raskolnikov, somehow find solace, even love, and, beyond that, a kind of redemptive sense of worth (so, too, with Dickens's dissolute ones, such as Sydney Carton). Unsurprisingly, these are individuals recognizable to us of the Western bourgeoisie, men and women not unlike Freud's patients, who also manage to find *their* kind of "redemption"—in the course of psychiatric treatment, for example, when a doctor's insights with respect to the reasons for their troubled state of mind get turned into narrative presentations on his part of their stories. That is a substantial part, actually, of what psychoanalysis is: the doctor "reads" the patient's life, assembles it into a rendered narrative, with the patient becoming, in turn, his or her reader, a listener to what an observer of himself or herself has come to know. All of this is idiosyncratic, personal: each man or woman is "driven" by particular interests, passions, a particular sense of what is suitable, what is undesirable, if not unseemly, or utterly out of order. "The mix in every patient I see is in certain important respects unique," Anna Freud once commented at the end of a challenging clinical seminar, and by "mix" she meant that human particularity: a person's life as it develops in a home, a neighborhood, a nation, in the midst of a historical time—this sum of "variables" prompting the formation of the mind's life, bearing down on it, giving it a distinctive, expressive existence.

For Orwell, the worried futurist, and Milosz, the dismayed observer, that psychological state of affairs had seemingly changed. For them, the state threatened to become not only militarily and politically triumphant, but psychologically so: the custodial Superego for millions, their Ids effectively enthralled, their Egos an instrument, pure and simple, of the state's bureaucratic manipulation. To be sure, philosophers such as Gabriel Marcel had claimed to glimpse a parallel, if not quite similar, sociological and psychological drama taking place in the advanced industrial nations of the West— so-called mass-men, individuals by the millions who are "alienated," who live for and by the slogans of a commercial world become powerfully persuasive. But totalitarian rule is quite another matter, Orwell believed, and Milosz declared out of a right as a witness to draw on comparative experiences. Milosz struggled (against the high and understandable odds of political despair) for balance, for nuance. Throughout *The Captive Mind* he wants to distinguish the inclination any of us has to one or another kind of personal, social, cultural, religious compliance (our conscience influenced by various others, by institutional life as it connects with our day-to-day experience) from the extraordinary nature of the Nazi state, the Soviet state, as they both pressed, by carefully developed design, on the lives of millions, using modern technology in a continuing public theater that made the religious theater of the past pale in comparison, and using, too, the full coercive power available to modern dictators and their fawning, fearful intimates.

Milosz starts his book, though, not with factual description but with relatively obscure literary discussion. The first chapter is titled "The Pill of Multi-Bing," which, we are told, has to do with "a curious book" that was published in Warsaw in 1932, a generation before Milosz set to work on *The Captive Mind.* The book's title is *Insatiability,* a two-volume novel by Stanislaw Witkiewicz, a Polish philosopher, who was also a painter. A phenomenologist, in the spirit of Husserl, Witkiewicz wondered what, if anything, made modern man "happy." Like many writers and artists and philosophers of the early decades of the twentieth century, he regarded civilization as a paradox: it provides both food and food for thought in substantial amounts, but it leaves many feeling insignificant, dwarfed by buildings, factories, social institutions to which they feel little affiliation, while also bereft of spiritual belief, because religion has been effectively "demythologized," not necessarily through study, reflection, argument, but by a general awareness of "science" and its conclusions that cuts deeply, decisively into the old assertions and certainties learned in Sunday School, Hebrew School.

In *Insatiability*, the phenomenon conveyed by the book's title is addressed through a storyteller's bold leap into imaginative fantasy, but, significantly, of a kind that possesses its own obvious ties to the mainstay of credibility in the West: materialism as the one hope that we still uphold with conviction, or that we won't cast aside, no matter our reservations or doubts—in this instance, the materialism of the omnipresent pill, ever ready to help us calm down, go to sleep, stay awake, digest our food, be rid of our waste, alleviate our headaches, toothaches, stomach pains, our myalgias and arthralgias. Milosz summarizes the thrust of *Insatiability* by noting that it initially describes people as "unhappy in that they have no faith and no sense of meaning in their work." He tells the Western readers of *The Captive Mind*, well aware of what has befallen him and his fellow Poles under the Soviet shadow, that in the pages of *Insatiability* "hawkers appear in the city peddling Multi-Bing pills." Those pills are named for a Mongolian philosopher, Multi-Bing (the long-standing European fear of invasion from the East!), and they, not tanks and airplanes, will become vehicles of conquest: those who ingest Multi-Bing, hitherto apathetic, perplexed, melancholy, become rather quickly "serene and happy." People apprehensive, agitated, become calm, even-tempered. The "dissonant music" of the past gives way to stirring "marches and odes." Abstract paintings are replaced by "socially useful pictures": a complete turn in a reigning culture. (The novel's author, upon learning that Stalin's army had invaded Poland from the east, on September 17, 1939, committed suicide.)

We are being told, right off, by Milosz, that art can foresee history, that there are clues in a culture that enable an all too accurate imaginative portrayal of what awaits us around time's corner. Armies matter, but their ultimate victory, Milosz and others have known, will depend on some solid social and psychological control over any given country's people. A writer's fantasy indicates a likely direction of history. The mind will be controlled not by a military presence, or even the persuasive influence of an ideological presence, but by dint of a mood-altering pill: people become compliant and passive in the face of history's unfolding struggles, a version of Orwell's worried prophecy, but one that specifies "neurochemistry" as the ultimate "force."

Yesterday's futurists have a way of becoming today's engineers, scientists, practical, technological experimenters. Jules Verne's *Twenty Thousand Leagues under the Sea*, the comic strip "Flash Gordon," or, for that matter, the visual and visionary ruminations of Leonardo da Vinci as he put them to paper, have become our submarines and airplanes and spaceships. Surely those machines will have their successors, and this planet will become a home base for further and farther penetrations of space by us, who will come to think of ourselves as, among other things, earth-folk, defined not only by, say, our nationalist but by our planetary origins. But right now we are not only exploring our moon and Mars and Saturn, gazing at greater stretches of the universe; we are also looking more confidently, knowingly, within ourselves—a huge jump taken this century by medical scientists. The brain, which has so successfully explored all other organs, and has, of course, imagined us doing so much, then enabled us to do so much here on Earth and elsewhere across the galaxy, is only recently, as mentioned, becoming able to understand itself with a similar kind of precision and competence. Such a development, the brain probing itself, learning to regulate itself, has also been the subject of substantial futurist speculation, Witkiewicz's meditation being one of many. Nor has an ominous, devouring, cruelly arbitrary Stalinism been the only political or economic system that has prompted such leaps of fancy with respect to the human mind: efforts, really, to conjure up a kind of "exit" for people very much threatened or vulnerable.

Perhaps the best-known novel, in that tradition, is Aldous Huxley's *Brave New World* (1932), wherein the drug "soma" figures as part of a broader scheme to strip people of their human nature, really, the strains they feel as members of a family, a workplace, a neighborhood, the worries they feel as they try to get along with their husbands or wives, their children, their bosses or employees, their fellow workers. Huxley has his laboring men and women swallowing tabs of "soma," reciting prayers; he introduces them to "hypnopedic conditioning," grants them sex on demand, and the result is a placid, quiescent employee—exactly what factory managers in our industrial nations need, want, expect of our assembly-line workers. Huxley's satire was directed at a mentality that upheld such mass production, with its human consequences. The motto for the people who live in that "new world" of his is "Community,

Identity, Stability," and the implication is that some-how, sometime ahead, through a mix of neurophysiol-ogy and political sociology we will be able to bring peo-ple around to the demands of advanced capitalism (or socialism, for that matter): turn them into willing, com-petent agents and instruments of an efficient "produc-tive society."

In a lesser literary vein, there is Philip K. Dick's *Blade Runner* (eventually made into a movie), which appeared in 1968. As the book opens, "a merry little surge of elec-tricity" is being "piped by automatic alarm from the mood organ" located near the character Rick Deckard's bed. As he awakens under such mind-galvanizing cir-cumstances, he turns to his nearby wife: "You set your Penfield too weak." He volunteers to reset it, but she wants no part of his initiative. In a few lines, the novel-ist draws on past neurological research (the Canadian scientist Wilder Penfield did pioneering explorations of the brain's functional life); he describes a future in which we manipulate our cognitive and emotional life through machines (or medicines); but he also, quite shrewdly, maybe more so than some of his "betters" among prophetic storytellers, indicates what may be left standing, so to speak, of our present psychological life, centuries from now, when all the advances in our knowledge of the brain have resulted in all those drugs and mechanical devices: namely, our own idiosyncratic, fussy, feisty selves, which, after all, may well have some say in what use we make of such a collective and avail-able "progress." Who, even then, in that future awaiting us, will use what in which manner? Human possibility will become enhanced, but human nature still could have some impact upon how (and when) that possibility is summoned: for what purposes, with whom, and how—or so a novelist not unable to leap across the generations, the centuries, even the millennia, nevertheless wants us to think. It is as if a radical futurist refuses to shed an obstinately conservative side of himself that insists on remembering our capacity as individuals to choose, to disagree as well as comply, to have our own, private opinions, attitudes, even with respect to what others eagerly embrace as necessary, salutary.

In any event, Dick's relatively recent science fiction has been followed by an utterly unsurprising *Time* cover story, titled "How Mood Drugs Work . . . and Fail," such a "news story," obviously, prompted by the increasingly "biological" nature of psychiatry. How well, in that regard, I remember the arrival of Thorazine when I was a house officer at the Massachusetts General Hospital, in the middle 1950s. How well, too, I remember one of my supervisors, Carl Binger, then editor of the journal *Psychosomatic Medicine*, telling me that there would be more and more such drugs, and that "one day" they would be (I still remember his choice of words) "elegant levers" for us doctors to grasp—a source of professional capability then way beyond the imagining of many of us. As if to give his predictive remarks a present-day sanction, Dr. Binger referred me to Freud's *Beyond the Pleasure Principle*, to this portion of it, which he let me know he knew well enough almost to quote by heart: "Biology is truly a land of unlimited possibilities. We may expect it to give us the most surprising information and we cannot guess what answers it will return in a few dozen years to the questions we have put to it. They may be of a kind which will blow away the whole of our artificial structure of hypotheses."

For Dr. Binger, the important point, then, as we conversed, was not only a coming biological ascendancy to psychiatry and psychoanalysis, and not only, too, Freud's willingness to look with some wry distance at his own ideas and, unlike some of his followers, see them in a historical context, but, most especially, his thoroughgoing hopefulness, of a kind almost immediate in its expectant expression: "a few dozen years"— that span of time from someone himself then in his sixties, a recent onlooker of a terribly destructive world war with disastrous social and economic consequences all too evident in Vienna, among other places. Still, the "first psychoanalyst," as Erik H. Erikson once called him, was quite able to foresee, within a century or so, the passing of his entire way of thinking, not to mention, presumably, the profession it had generated, "the last psychoanalyst" soon enough a personal and chronological reality. Moreover, I remember so clearly Dr. Binger's agreement with Freud's assessment of things: "You will live to see psychoanalysis hemmed in, further and further, by biology, as Freud predicted, and you will live to see sociology also bearing down on psychoanalysis." I wrote those words down as those of a psychoanalytic supervisor of mine, but at the time I had no confidence that I had ahead of me the kind of longevity Dr. Binger was positing as mine.

Yet in two dozen of those "few dozen" years Freud mentioned, I would, indeed, see the relative demise of the "orthodox" psychoanalysis I knew as a young psychiatrist in Boston; would see the increasing realization by my colleagues of the persuasive role race and class and ethnicity and nationality and culture and history all play in our mind's thinking, feeling; and would, finally, begin to see what Dr. Binger meant when, back in 1960, he spoke about "biological psychiatry" as just ahead of us. Indeed, the career of a friend of mine, who once taught at Harvard Medical School and now works at the Rockefeller Institute in New York City, is an example of how one professional life can more than accommodate itself to such a shift in a profession's direction. Torsten Wiesel was born in Sweden, was educated there, learned to be a child psychiatrist there. Eventually, however, he came to the United States and learned to do neurobiological research—for which he would win a Nobel Prize: a pioneer in biochemical and physiological and anatomical research in the human brain, assisted, of course, through the study of the brains of animals.

Another physician who has concentrated his thinking on such matters, though as a novelist rather than laboratory researcher, is Walker Percy, whose *Love in the Ruins* has already been mentioned. For all his prophecies of social collapse, moral confusion, Dr. Percy nevertheless flirts with a new science able to bring the brain's functions under closer scrutiny than is now the case. The novel is comic (in a serious, even quite sad way); the reader is offered a "lapsometer," meant to take (literally) the measure of the mind's psychological, if not spiritual or reflective, state: a neurobiological instrument that is both diagnostic and therapeutic. We are prompted to think about not only where we're headed, but where we'll soon enough be. Meanwhile, in 1997, while reading the journal *Psychoanalysis and Contemporary Thought*, I came upon an article with the title "Proposals regarding the Neurobiology of Oedipality," a title I could imagine Dr. Percy's using in mild jest a quarter of a century ago, a means (back then) of spoofing, perhaps, a bloated psychoanalytic vocabulary and an all too insipid or inadequate neurobiological one: neither field able to call upon the other in any useful way then foreseeable. But the essay is written with confidence, draws upon established research as well as speculation. We are introduced, really, to the neural networks that form the anatomical basis of our emotional life, and we are reminded that there is a developmental neuroanatomy that parallels the developmental psychology which we have learned (in certain precincts of our Western world) to call "oedipal." Put all too succinctly, nerves are acquiring their myelin just as young children are learning how to get on with their mothers, fathers.

Not that this article is meant to be a breakthrough one; there is so much we *don't* know about the development of thinking, never mind the specifics of this or that (hypothetical) "complex." But the effort, at this point, in a psychoanalytic publication to connect what Freud himself called a "metapsychology" to neuroanatomy is itself a step in what I suppose can be called an emerging biological psychoanalysis. Further along (a few more of those "dozens of years" Dr. Freud mentioned, a century or two of them, maybe), we will have some idea, at a more microcosmic level, of the neurochemistry and neurophysiology of our thinking life—and then, plausibly, the specifics (with respect to children) of maternal attachment, of rivalry, or fear in connection with fathers, will be ours to figure out in a cellular mode: the biochemistry and neurophysiology of certain localized areas of the brain.

As I say the above, I realize—the article just mentioned notwithstanding, and all the mind-altering drugs which have recently become part of the psychiatric armamentarium also notwithstanding—that we have the proverbial "miles to go," ever so many of them, before we will know about the brain what the brain has enabled us to know, for instance, about the pancreas or the kidneys or the lungs: their structure and function at a microcosmic level, a biochemical and physiological level. Still, to call upon psychoanalytic theory in a way different from that of Dr. Forsyth, an anthropologist at the University of Southern Colorado, in the above cited article on "neurobiology and oedipality," the coming centuries of this dawning third millennium will gradually give us a new kind of Ego, one with real authority, with power to act, rather than primarily react (Freud's early view of things). Sometime in this new millennium, one suspects, our space-people will multiply, the planets of this solar system will yield many of their secrets, and (who knows?) we will figure out ways to plunge into the further recesses (from our viewpoint) of the infinity that surrounds us. But we will also come into growing command of our "thoughts," our "emotions": what we call the Id and the Superego will be understood biologically and, thereafter, brought under control. Once futurists pictured the Superego as an instrument of a state's political authority, an Ego thereby endlessly vulnerable to public slogans become individual mandates, compulsions—the stuff of bureaucratic suppression, repression. Eventually, there will be an Ego able to be its own master, relatively unassailed from within and free to assert itself with an unprecedented competence that is grounded in neurochemical knowledge and its application: biology rather than state power as psychologically triumphant.

Obviously, it is impossible to know how our future psychopharmacological capabilities will effect our emotional (or social or political) destiny. The coming centuries will offer their very own version of Freud's drama, with its three well-known protagonists. But, as Freud anticipated, "mind" will increasingly become "matter," a move from metapsychological inquiry to medical applications and interventions tied to a materialist comprehension of how the brain works. Already biochemistry (in the form of lithium and other drugs) has brought manic-depressive illness under some substantial degree of control; and already the drugs that work against schizophrenia's symptoms, or, indeed, the anxieties and mood disorders of more "normal" people, have generated not only a large medical literature but a cultural response, and, too, among those who take this or that pill, a personal, introspective response—the observant Ego at work. Here, for instance, is a fourth-year medical student speaking of her bouts of anxiety and depression, her use of Prozac and Paxil, but, more generally, her sense of what the future holds for human beings as science gives them more and more leverage over nature, including their thinking and feeling lives: "Sometimes I wonder whether we won't outdo ourselves—learn how to do so much that 'we' are left behind! What do I mean? [I was quick to ask.] I don't know. The subject is too big even for words—that's what I mean! One day we'll even know how people get to speak or write— we'll be able to 'control' that the same way we control the functions of other organs, don't you think? Isn't that the logic of where we're headed? I hear neurobiologists talk about the brain's 'properties' and its 'purpose' or 'qualities' or 'functions' the way we talk about the heart, its 'purposes' and 'functions,' or the G.I. tract or the liver and kidneys—and why not! It's mind-boggling—excuse the way I put it!—but it's going to happen: we'll know the neurobiology of thinking and writing. I mean, we'll understand all that down to the level of tissues and cells and biochemistry and physiology—neurochemistry and neurophysiology way beyond anything we now know. I wouldn't even know how to think about what we'll know about all this someday: what we'll know about knowing, I guess you could say!

"One thing I wonder about—will there always be a 'me' who wonders about what she's doing, and why, or will the 'me' or the 'you' get lost in all the understanding or control we have over the way the brain works. I know I'm not being clear here—I'm being philosophical about what the biological achievements in brain research will mean for us way in the future, a few hundred years from now. Even now, there are times when I wonder where 'I' begin and all the machines and medicines stop—especially when I look at my grandmother and my mom and dad, and me! My grandmother has lived into her middle eighties, and she's lucky, she's practically never been sick. She doesn't take pills. She wakes up on her own—no alarm clock. She drives, but she prefers to walk. She *writes* letters. She has a gas stove and a refrigerator, but no microwave. She uses the phone, but she says she hates talking on it 'too long'!

"My dad—he wakes up by an alarm. He picks up messages by the phone while he's having breakfast. He has his laptop computer near him in the kitchen, and his fax. In his car he has a phone and a fax. He'll hold the wheel with one hand, and talk on the phone, or get his faxes, or dictate. He goes and talks with people all over the world, sometimes, in a teleconference place. He has an 'alarm' in his watch, to remind him that it's time to do this, or something else. He takes pills for headaches, for heartburn, for his nerves; and sometimes, to get to sleep. He flies all over and has all kind of routines to fight jet lag. For him the cellular phone and the laptop are constant necessities—like my grandma carrying her handbag, with her wallet and handkerchief and some lipstick and a small mirror!

"I'm my dad's daughter—and I rely on all the gadgets he does, and I'm sure there will be more of them in the twenty-first century. I've grown *up* with all this; my dad grew *into* it all. He remembers when the fax machine first came out; and the computers and cellular phones. He jokes—he remembers when the doctors had, maybe, phenobarbital to calm you down or knock you out! My grandma shakes her head when she hears him talk like that. Once, she said we'll all get 'lost'—we'll become 'slaves' of all the 'gadgets,' all the 'machines,' all the 'medicines they have.' 'What would happen if we had to exist without that stuff?'; she asked that, and Dad and I laughed. 'Back to nature,' Dad joked—we'd go back to our 'original state.' I kept thinking of that later; I wondered if I could get through a day if I didn't have all that 'stuff,' an alarm clock, my 'psychotropic drugs,' the fax and the computer and the cellular phone. What will it be like a few hundred years from now—will people read books anymore? Will we 'ingest' knowledge, by pill, by some machine? This sounds weird and crazy and fantastic—but my grandmother says that if she'd been told when she was my age what the world would be like when she got to be eighty-five, she'd have thought the person telling her all that had 'quite a wild imagination!'"

We both are smiling—the concreteness of that sixty or so span of years just mentioned seizes our attention, makes us time-conscious, and especially so now, in early 1997, in the last years of a century, a millennium, a time of looking forward and, as well, a time of remembering. A history of science major, now headed for a career in "research medicine," she admits to a "philosophical side" and wonders whether such a way of using the mind won't, itself, become outmoded, a relic of a distant past: "Everything is so *functional* these days. My dad says he's glad—he doesn't have any time to waste, and all of the 'gadgets' my grandmother mentions are huge time-savers. He can't imagine being without them, and I can't either. Down the line, what other 'gadgets' will become indispensable? Won't all that have an effect on the human mind? I mean, is there a limit to how fast we can think and act? It won't be long before we'll be able to 'rocket' rather than fly to

Tokyo or Johannesburg—that means we'll be places in minutes, not hours. It won't be long before we look at each other while we talk on the phone. Right now, you can reach some people anywhere—they're never 'away,' if they don't want to be. I'm just talking about the technology we have, not the technology that's coming. Maybe we'll fly to work in our 'cars'! Maybe we'll press buttons to shop—well, we already can do that. Is there a point that we'll reach—when we'll be overwhelmed, when our bodies, our brains, say 'no,' it's more than we can take? I guess things come just slow enough—the new technology—for us to get used to the latest breakthrough. But I wonder whether our ability to invent and discover won't outreach, surpass our ability to live with what we've done [built, designed, and manufactured].

"I guess if we try to imagine what it'll be like a couple of centuries from now, or at the start of the *fourth* millennium, we should try to think about our limits as well as our ability to overcome limits: I mean, the difference between what we can do with our brains in the way of figuring things out and building technology that will take full advantage of what we've figured out [on the one hand] and [on the other hand] what our brains can 'take.' I mean, I can imagine some neurophysiologist discovering *why* we need to sleep, what sleep does for the brain, and then discovering some substance that 'replaces' sleep—do you see what I mean?—and then we'd all be strutting around, telling each other that we've just added on a third of our lives to our 'living time,' because sleep isn't necessary any more. Just think of that!

You're shaking your head and smiling, but that could be happening sometime in the future—and then time itself will change: we'll be living so much longer, and we'll be awake so much longer. I wonder how it will affect us, the way we *are*, not the way we *live*, or is this kind of question, this kind of thinking, going to be obsolete, because we'll be able to 'get rid of it,' 'control' what we think as well as control 'craziness,' 'bad thoughts,' depression and anxiety?"

We are now both speechless and, in a way, exhausted with respect to our ability to think further about what has just been thought! Her mind (I *do* think) has raced so far into the future, tried to imagine so vividly where we are headed, that we have gone beyond our practical ability to fill in the blanks, so to speak—catch up with the fantasy by dealing concretely with the details, the day-to-day consequences of such an outcome. Can we eventually "program" our behavior, so that our emotions recede in significance to our cognitive life, as it connects with technology, becomes not only the heart of what we do, but the very essence of who we are? This medical student was worried about being "lost," and as she kept telling me that, I recalled Walker Percy's phrase "lost in the cosmos," a title he gave to a book of essays he wrote, but also a phrase he used to describe our sense of our situation, our condition: this creature of consciousness who through language tries to comprehend the mysteries of time and space, those two infinities in which we for a while are immersed. But one day words such as "consciousness" and "language" will also yield their meaning to biological investigation, and who can know for sure what the implications and the results of such inquiry will be for us; that is, how our sense of the world, and of our ourselves, and how our capacity to connect with others, to communicate, to ask and to tell, will all be altered!

As that student prepares to leave my university office, she asks me, casually, whether I "still believe in psycho-analysis." She is smiling, knows the irony of the inquiry, given our hour-long leap into both the darkness and light of the time ahead of us. I respond with a demurral, insist that psychoanalysis is not something to be "be-lieved in"; rather, it is one more way of seeing things in a long chain of such that extends over the many cen-turies, millennia of our thinking, reflecting life. But then, she shrewdly amplifies her question and, by more than implication, corrects me. She wants me to think of psychoanalysis as a "metaphor," rather than a psycho-logical theory, or kind of "therapy." A metaphor for what? "For people trying to get to know each other, learn from each other, for human connection," she says, and then reminds me of Martin Buber's phrase "I-Thou." She is hoping, she insists, maybe hoping against hope, she acknowledges, that amidst all the "progress" which will arrive over the generations to follow hers, all the knowledge about, yes, knowledge itself (the biology of knowledge become part of knowledge!), there will still be in those people who inhabit this planet ideas, ideals, passions (Ego, Superego, Id) that are no more regarded reductively, courtesy of biology, than they are considered reductively by many thoughtful psychoana-lysts today, in the name of psychology. We pursue that matter a bit, notwithstanding her need to leave to put

in time in a research lab. She worries that with an increasing rationality, grounded in a knowing command
of the brain's manner of working, what we now call
"love" or even "goodness" or "badness" or, ironically,
"scientific research" will all be explained, defined, and
put under some control: a presently wild notion that
seems worthy of drugstore paperback fiction, but not
beyond a comprehension based on the assumption of
biochemistry and physiology as the ultimate owners, it
can be said, of the brain and, just as ultimately, the
property of us who, after all, have founded and built
those two bodies of knowledge, whose dominion can
only grow and grow as time goes by.

So it will be, we muse—an increasingly "biochemical
Ego"; that is, we will extend our knowing authority over
our psychological life, which is an aspect of our brain's
activity. Even as the brain controls our breathing, our
seeing, our hearing, it also controls our thinking and
feeling, hence the future of our biological inquiry into
cortical activity: a realization on our part of what takes
place as we, say, do brain research. One can imagine,
then, a biochemical self-consciousness: the surveillance
on our part of cortical activity, of the brain's neurophysiological activity, that extends even to the research
effort itself, even as now certain individuals monitor
their psychological state, and what they are doing, and
where, and under which circumstances, so that they
may take this medication at this dose, or another medication at another dose.

The secular mind in the past lived side by side with
the spiritual interests and yearnings of millions, a sacred
mind. In recent centuries that secular mind has itself

experienced a transformation. Once an alternative to entrenched religious life, that secularity became an aspect of individualism, as societies became less and less dominated by church life, more and more capitalistic in nature: the emergence of the bourgeoisie, with its tastes and preferences and interests very much "of this world." In this century Fascism, Nazism, Communism gave us a taste of the state as an overwhelming presence in the mental life of millions, a major presence in the indoctrinated thinking of a nation's people, especially its children (the Hitler Youth, the Komsomol). With totalitarianism on the wane, the nations of the world look ahead, now, to a future of discovery and growth rather than wars of conquest (and wars within nations), the murderous persecution of some by others. With any luck, that "discovery" will include scientific exploration of a kind that will, at last, give us knowing access to our own nature as explorers, discoverers: mind investigating brain, and, thereby, Emerson's "thinking man" a sovereign as never before in his native land, the head—able to comprehend it as he once took the measure of all those foreign territories that stretch downward from the brain stem toward the chest cavity, the abdomen.

Such a biological achievement will, in one sense, as Freud suggested, "blow away" traditional psychological and philosophical notions of human experience. Yet, as that medical student kept trying to suggest, we will, in certain important respects, still each be a self, not only the one who will master the brain, and thereby the mind, but also the one who knows hope and disappointment, love and loss: the one who can smile and cry, who can take pride in what has been achieved and see it for its limits, as a mere part of a larger story. No doubt, then, the biochemical Ego, as it were, will have its important bearing on what we can be and do, on how we live with ourselves and others, but at the same time we will surely be the mass of "biochemical processes," of "continuing neurophysiological activity," that has been plumbed as never before, but that also is capable of listening to Beethoven or Billie Holiday or Bruce Springsteen, capable of reading George Eliot or Leo Tolstoy or Chekhov or Raymond Carver or Flannery O'Connor or Walker Percy, capable of looking at Rembrandt and Van Gogh and Munch and Hopper, and capable of being such individuals, too—therein the Ego as a visitor to countless countries, a bearer of many names, an accomplished traveler able figuratively as well as literally to cross oceans, continents, time zones, ever anxious to learn more but, also, to figure out what that learning means in the larger scheme of things.

Put differently, we are the creature in whom knowing, clearly, has its greatest distinction. Other creatures know reflexively; we know tentatively, haltingly as children, then searchingly as youths, and finally, some of us, with the confident stride of, say, a Freud or of a future neurobiologist who will tell us exactly how a Freud thinks, exactly where in the brain ideas have their origin, and how they come about: the anatomy of thinking, the biochemistry of thinking. So with feeling, too—the knowing with respect to feeling awaits us: where it occurs, how it gets generated in us, and how it connects us with thoughts, ideas, interests, not to mention activities. Here, at this time, it is almost impossible for us to get *there*—to know the details and implications of a future in which we have fathomed structurally and functionally, so to speak, the nature of language, of thought, of feeling: the brain, at last, the mind's true domain. Still, the logic of materialism, and our proven capabilities as they inform our restlessly exploring nature, lead us in that direction, foretell our eventual arrival: the secular mind as ever wondering, probing, as ever intent on mastery.

In that long run of our history such knowing is, perhaps, our (secular) destiny; and yet, as some future philosopher will surely remind our triumphant biologists of the brain, there is knowing and there is knowing about the place of knowing in the course of the lived, the experienced, life: knowing and being as brothers, or sisters, but not as identical twins. Knowing is a part of being; being without knowing is, with respect to our humanity, not being. We know (and know and know); we feel, and knowing connects to that feeling, can prompt it or respond to it, so we psychiatrists notice all the time—and then there is the "leap" of action, of being carried to another kind of affirmation. Even with an almost (from our present perspective) infinite expansion of such knowing (such knowing about knowing, about feeling), we will always be, too, the creature of action, of commitment to deeds, not to mention one another, or so one hopes, even prays (the last gasp of the sacred). One prays at the very least on behalf of one's kind, though unsure, in a secular sense, to whom or what such prayer is directed, other than, needless to say, one's own secular mind, ever needy of an "otherness" to

address through words become acts of appeal, of worried alarm, of lively and grateful expectation: please, oh
please, let things go this way, and not in that direction—the secular mind given introspective, moral
pause, its very own kind of sanctity.